HUNTING WITH THE
HAWKS

Untold stories from the elite
South African crime-fighting unit

GRAHAM COETZER

Tafelberg

Tafelberg
An imprint of NB Publishers, a Division of Media24 Boeke (Pty) Ltd
40 Heerengracht, Cape Town
www.tafelberg.com

Cover design: Nudge Studio
Book design: Marthie Steenkamp
Editing: Angela Voges
Proofreading: Glynne Newlands

Printed and bound by CTP Printers, Cape Town

First edition, fourth impression 2024

ISBN: 978-0-624-09356-5
Epub: 978-0-624-09357-2

For my parents, David and Caroline –
no son could have asked for better.

To my gorgeous wife Louise, the love of my life.

Finally, to my beautiful daughters Shelby and Hayley,
two souls who remind me that there is
always light amidst the darkness.

Contents

Preface

As an investigative journalist, it's easy to develop a cynical view of the police, especially in a country like South Africa. I've covered stories where police members themselves have been accused of extremely serious crimes: corruption, extortion, kidnapping and even murder, to name just a few.

So, this is not a book masquerading as a PR exercise for the Directorate for Priority Crime Investigation (DPCI). Known to most of us as the Hawks, the DPCI is an agency within the South African Police Service (SAPS) that targets organised crime, economic crime and corruption. Founded in 2008, the Hawks have had their fair share of ups and downs.

But within the organisation, some men and women have dedicated their lives to combating criminals. The kind of cops who, despite a lack of funding and resources, get up every morning and try to make a difference in a country where the odds are often stacked against them. Due to the nature of their work, we, as the public, hardly ever get to hear first-hand accounts of their stories. Despite often risking their lives for us, they get very little recognition.

I hope that by offering you this glimpse behind the scenes into a world seldom observed by the glare of the media spotlight, I've been able to give a little credit where credit is due.

1

PROJECT MADAME

The young girl has her head bowed. Humiliated. Scared. Deep down inside, she's angry at herself. For letting them do this to her. They've used her. Abused her.

She's seen more than most during her sixteen short years of life.

She'd never met her father. Didn't even know if he was still alive or in jail. He was serving time for murder. Her mother had eventually also been locked up. Drugs.

Left to fend for herself, she soon saw the uglier side of Cape Town. The side they don't show you on the tourist websites or in-flight magazines. The side run by gangs and criminal syndicates. The cold, hard streets where alcohol and narcotics offered the only escape from a violent and unfair reality.

At first, she'd thought they were her friends. They'd taken her in. Offered her a bed to sleep in. A roof over her head. They'd shared their seemingly never-ending supply of stash with her. Whisky. Vodka. And then the better stuff. Coke. Meth. Heroin.

You name it, they had it. It seemed only fair that they'd asked her to help them. Told her how she could earn her keep. She was young. Men would pay well to spend time with her. They would worship her body.

After the first few times, it all seemed very normal. Besides, her friends would give her whatever she asked for afterwards to take her mind off things. Shame? Guilt? Disgust? The answers could be found at the bottom of a bottle or the end of a needle.

But soon, her friends were no longer friendly. What started as one or two men a week suddenly became a dozen every day. What her friends had given freely, she now had to pay for. And no matter how many clients she pleased or how humiliating the indignities she suffered at their hands, she never seemed to make enough.

Her friends worshipped money. She had to make more.

She'd considered leaving. But she knew they would find her. She'd seen it happen to others. Disobeying meant punishment.

And so, she sat there. Her head bowed. Waiting. At last, he entered the room. He was one of them. Her friends. But she knew better now. They called him the enforcer.

Yesterday, she'd left the house for a few minutes without permission. She'd needed a box of tampons and a packet of cigarettes. She'd been gone for less than half an hour.

Today, she would pay for her sins.

During the research for this book, I was prepared to be given some appalling insights into the underbelly of South African crime. As an investigative journalist, you like to tell yourself you've seen the worst humanity has to offer.

In any given week, you might be listening to an elderly lady's gut-wrenching story of how she inadvertently sunk her savings into buying a home, only to find out the property developer was a ruthless fraud who'd left her destitute. Or seeing a husband break down after sharing his tale of being unable to protect his wife when they were not only hijacked by men masquerading as police officers on the highway but also kidnapped, held at gunpoint for hours on end, and forced to hand over their ATM PINs and bank cards so that the gang could clean out their accounts. Sadly, South Africa has a lot to offer regarding crime stories. And the list of cases I've looked into gets progressively darker: torture, rape, murder . . .

So, on a rainy Western Cape morning, when I walked into the Bellville offices of the Directorate for Priority Crime Investigation's Organised Crime Unit to discuss a human trafficking case, I was ready for bad. Even really bad. After all, I'd heard it all before. But nothing quite prepares you for the sheer levels of debasement of humanity when you start delving into the depths of the global scourge of human trafficking. The story behind the investigation that the Hawks codenamed 'Project Madame' is no exception.

The old South African Revenue Service (SARS) building on the corner of Market and AJ West streets, which currently houses several Western Cape Hawks' units, cuts an imposing figure into the Bellville skyline. It screams law enforcement. But once you're inside the building, it is a sore reminder that the South African Police Service is an institution in dire financial straits. Annual budget cuts over the past few years have made the thin blue line ever thinner, as one news outlet quipped. So, along with overall low morale and a seemingly never-ending list of police corruption cases flooding South African headlines every other week, the men and women in blue who want to do their best often have to do so with outdated equipment and make themselves at home in ageing infrastructure.

The interior of the old building is no exception. It's in desperate need of a new paint job, at the very least. A new everything. Entering the lifts is an act of faith. When they're working, that is. The SAPS has not been spared the frustrations of the rolling electricity blackouts imposed by the besieged national power provider, Eskom. This is the unfortunate state of affairs at most police stations and buildings across the country.

A first-time visitor to the heart of South Africa's most elite crime-fighting unit's Western Cape offices could be forgiven for being less than awe-inspired. And it doesn't get any better in other provinces.

I'd flown down to Cape Town to meet Captain Lizelle Herbst, a woman with 31 years of law enforcement experience under her belt. All but one of those years were spent in specialised units. And within minutes of meeting her, she'd brightened up the gloomy atmosphere I'd felt, probably brought on by the weather and the building.

On appearance alone, she's certainly not what you'd call the stereotypical cop. Like most Hawks' members, she doesn't come to work in uniform. When we first met, she was wearing a flower-print top and matching skirt. Immaculately manicured fingernails had been decorated in shades of red, pink and white, sporting tiny pearl decorations. The look was completed by a colourful pair of horn-rimmed glasses that framed a set of ocean-green eyes. Those eyes light up when she gets passionate recalling past cases, and they offer the only real clue to the iron resolve beneath her otherwise genial appearance.

Before joining the DPCI's human trafficking team, she'd cut her teeth in their anti-gang unit. Anyone in the know will tell you that investigating gang-related crime in the Western Cape is no joke. And, as I'm sure Captain Herbst would agree, neither is human trafficking.

One of the first things she told me over a cup of coffee she'd jokingly 'ordered' her partner, Captain Gerhard Kotze, to make us, has stuck with me: 'Human trafficking isn't just about what our success rate in court is going to be; it's about every single person we can save. That's a bonus point for us.'

That one statement tells you all you need to know about her devotion to the cause. It also encompasses my primary motivation for telling these stories: the SAPS – and, along with them, the Hawks – have acquired a bad rep in the media in recent years. Some of that is well deserved.

But few members of the public ever get to see behind the scenes where there are also some incredible successes in the fight against crime. Neither do we get to hear from the dedicated souls who, despite all the odds stacked against them, still make this country a safer place to live in. There are many of these unsung heroes among the police. Lizelle is undoubtedly one of them.

According to her, South Africa's leading human trafficking cases involve the sexual exploitation of people. In some countries, men, women and children are trafficked into forced manual labour. But we're a hotspot for the sex trade.

'Today, we are nothing other than milk or bread that can be bought on the shelves – with a shelf life. And unfortunately, when it comes to human trafficking, where sex is the exploitation, there is a shelf life connected to the victims. Like milk and bread that get old and rotten, victims are discarded once used. It's a terribly cruel world out there for our people who get caught up in human trafficking.'

For Lizelle, who was the investigating officer on Project Madame, the case started in 2017. Her team received numerous complaints about a brothel operating in an upmarket area of Cape Town. The residential house used as a cover for the brothel's activities was a mere five-minute drive from the world-famous views of Table Mountain that holidaymakers can enjoy at Bloubergstrand beach. Situated in the affluent Table View suburb (named after those same views), the brothel, by day, looked like any other house in the neighbourhood.

But at night, the place turned into every neighbour's worst nightmare: loud music, open drug use, and numerous violent altercations. Police were called to the scene every other week to break up the fights. The once-quiet suburb and its residents had reached a breaking point.

For Lizelle and the Hawks' team looking into the case, it was immediately apparent that there was more to the house than met the eye. Was a brothel being operated right under the noses of the residents of the picturesque suburb? The investigating team's suspicions were confirmed when their initial probe showed that the lessee was well known to the police.

'She had a previous conviction for operating a brothel. So, at that time, we had a pretty good idea that the information was true,' Lizelle said.

The woman, who would later become known to the Hawks as the kingpin in the Madame case, was Shantel Reyneke-Bridger. Her previous conviction for operating a brothel stemmed from an investigation run by no other than Lizelle's current partner in the Hawks, Captain Gerhard Kotze. In that case, the courts had given her a suspended sentence.

At the time, Reyneke-Bridger was 44 years old, a heavy-set woman whose greying hair was dyed blonde and worn long – falling to her hips when not tied up. In a mugshot of her in the Hawks' case files, she's wearing a grey sweater and staring at the camera with a deadpan expression. But the eyes . . . Her eyes in that picture seem as cold and callous as the nearby Atlantic Ocean when the weather turns ugly.

Through information gleaned from informants, Lizelle discovered that, instead of ending her life of crime after her previous run-in with the law, Reyneke-Bridger had upped her game and was now heading a brothel and a full-blown organised crime syndicate. But as any good detective (or journalist, for that matter) will tell you, information and gossip do not make a case.

The investigators soon put the Table View house under surveillance. Before infiltrating a crime syndicate, the police need to know as much about its operations as possible. Who are the role players, who's in charge, and who's making the money? In this case, the surveillance inevitably led them to the brothel's clientele. Vehicle number plates were recorded and clients were identified. Those same clients eventually provided much of the inside information the Hawks sought. Many of the men were married and not keen for their extramarital activities to become public knowledge. Like the little yellow Cape canaries you'd find in gardens all over Cape Town, they sang when confronted by the Hawks.

'It's one way to get as much information about the syndicate as possible,' Lizelle told me. 'Their MO [modus operandi], their movements, and of course who plays which role in the organisation.'

As the team continued their investigation, Reyneke-Bridger, perhaps getting wind of the ongoing surveillance, changed her MO. Abandoning the house in Table View, she spread the brothel across several venues in Cape Town. Small groups of the sex workers in her employ now operated from modest apartments rented by Shantel. She would only use an apartment for a few weeks before switching locations.

Prospective clients were lured to the venues by online sites. These web pages contain photos of the women on offer and a list of their services. Clients could reach them via cellphone numbers at the bottom of the pages. Scrolling through the case files and looking at the provocative images taken of the women to lure in the insatiable 'johns', I'm struck by a social dichotomy behind the case that bothers me to this day.

Yes, the people behind sex trafficking are abhorrent – bottom feeders who latch on to society's weak and vulnerable, exploiting them for personal gain. But they wouldn't be in business without a market for their tainted goods. Right now, across the world, men (and, you might be surprised to find out, quite a few women as well) are sitting behind the screens of their phones and laptops, combing through the same or similar websites. And, as if at some human cattle auction, deciding on what they'd like to buy. Small or big breasts? Blonde or brunette? Male, female, bi or transsexual? Willing to indulge in this bizarre fetish or that. Every possible fantasy is catered for. Everything's for sale at the great online human meat market. Available 24/7! Anything you want, as long as the price is right . . .

I've interviewed quite a few sex workers in my career. Trust me when I tell you that very few are in the business by choice. Even fewer can earn any decent living from it. And whether they fall into the legal definition of being trafficked or not, most of those I've met are victims. The johns who pay for their services may sleep better at night by reciting all the clichés – she's just a drug addict, a worthless whore, she chose this life – but make no mistake, they're as much a part of the problem as the organised crime syndicates that are all too often in control behind the scenes, profiting from that most human of the seven deadly sins: lust.

'The cellphone numbers of every girl on those sites went straight through to Shantel. So she handled the calls, made the bookings, and just let the ladies know when there was a client,' Lizelle told me.

While this was happening, the Hawks started looking at Reyneke-Bridger and her associates' phone records and bank statements. This would later play a crucial role in proving that the syndicate was a criminal enterprise being run solely for the profit of those involved. They needed to see who contacted whom, how often they spoke to each other, and where the money was going. All the background information eventually left investigators with a decent 'spidergram' – a diagram visually connecting the main suspects. Lizelle says this is a valuable tool in the investigator's arsenal.

'We could then, of course, determine the hierarchy of the syndicate. Shantel Reyneke-Bridger was our number one at that stage. The project was called Project Madame, which was a direct reference to her.'

Her right-hand man and boyfriend at the time was identified as 37-year-old Juan Warren. Another main suspect under investigation was Norman Bridger (31), Shantel's husband. Despite Shantel's ongoing romance with Juan, she and Norman had not divorced. The trio seemed to have a cosy relationship.

They were often seen together blowing vast amounts of money at casinos around the city, and even shared a home.

Also on the Hawks' radar were several 'heavies', men with brutal reputations employed as security for the syndicate's operations. They served dual purposes, protecting the sex workers from unruly clients but, more often than not, being used by Reyneke-Bridger to keep those same women in line. Minor infractions, such as leaving the brothel without permission, were punished with fines – sex workers were forced to pay these from their own pockets. Anything deemed a more serious offence by the syndicate would result in physical assaults on the women.

As investigators dug deeper, it became clear that Norman Bridger was running another division of the syndicate's operations. While involved in the daily management of the brothels, his role was to orchestrate a reign of terror against their clients. Whether using outright theft, fear and intimidation, or both, Bridger had set out to fleece his unwitting patrons of every last cent.

Some of his victims were 'lucky' – they only had cash or valuables stolen. Others kissed their cars goodbye. Many others also fell victim to the syndicate's 'sextortion' tactics. The term refers to victims of extortion who are intimidated into handing over large amounts of cash to criminals or risk having intimate photos or videos of themselves shared with friends and family. The threats also often include having embarrassing evidence published on social media sites for the whole world to see. Unfortunately for the victims of these crimes, once they've paid the syndicates, they're caught in a hole that will only get deeper. The extortionists will keep demanding money, and the victims will have to keep paying. I've encountered cases of men having lost everything – their homes, wives and jobs. For some of them, suicide offered the only way out. Lizelle remembers uncovering the extent of this side of the syndicate's activities and Bridger's role in it.

'He played the role of blackmailer and had a leg of the operation where they were involved with housebreaking and vehicle theft. While the sex workers were busy with the clients, the second leg of the syndicate moved in. They robbed the clients of their car keys; they stripped their houses of valuables. From the cellular communications we later obtained, you could see that the sex workers provided this side of the syndicate with all sorts of information. The person wears this kind of watch . . . there's this much money in the safe . . . so it was absolutely organised. This is where Norman Bridger came in. And he was also well known for the vehicles that he stole. The sex workers would often provide him with the remote or the key. Because the victims knew they were robbed while engaging with sex workers, many of these cases went unreported. In those cases where there were dockets, we went through each of them. In Norman Bridger's case, he was involved in 63 cases of house robberies and thefts. Not one of these cases were successfully prosecuted. The complainants were either threatened or refused to testify. And there was no further work done on those dockets.'

This allowed Shantel and Norman to get away with the thefts for years. Some sex workers were complicit in drugging their clients, allowing Norman even greater opportunities to extort them. At the time, a well-known party drug was becoming very popular in South Africa.

Gamma-hydroxybutyrate (GHB) – or liquid G, as it is known on the streets – is a so-called designer drug and is often found in nightclubs. Similar to ecstasy, liquid G takes effect rapidly when consumed orally and can leave users with anything from feelings of euphoria to powerful hallucinations. One of the main side effects is memory loss. A few drops of the colourless and odourless liquid slipped into an unwitting victim's drink could leave him incapacitated for hours. The sex workers would then take compromising photos or videos of their drugged victims. These included images of them in the nude, having sex, or, in one case, unconscious with a bottle of alcohol forced into his rectum.

The images and videos gave Norman all the necessary ammunition to extort his unfortunate victims. WhatsApp messages sent to the men and later obtained by the investigators showed the pressure they faced: *What will the mother of your children say and your daughter who so [sic] well known.* A few minutes later, that message was followed by: *Will she send me pics, goga. She has too, you know [sic] I like it. Will she take it? What will she do for me.* The threats were intended to put the fear of God into their recipients. And it worked. *I will put this on Facebook and share the whole world will know. Ten [R10 000] right nw [sic]. Then we close the book. That's meeting halfway.*

Unfortunately, the 'book' will never be closed when dealing with organised crime. I've covered these kinds of cases before. In almost all the 'sextortion' cases I've looked at, the criminals never stop. Once you've paid, you're in their clutches. The threats of exposure and the demands for cash will keep coming. In cases I've investigated, this has led to divorce, financial ruin and even suicide for the victims.

During Project Madame, Lizelle and her team would meet Mr X, the son of a prominent South African businessman.

Mr X fell victim to Shantel's crew after booking one of her sex workers, and he eventually handed over nearly R2,5 million to the syndicate to prevent his sexual exploits from being made public.

Once they'd gathered enough intelligence on the syndicate and their dealings, Lizelle's team had to devise a feasible plan to bring Project Madame to a successful conclusion.

'After Madame was registered as a project,' she told me, 'we sat and asked ourselves how to address it. When you've got a project on drugs or any other commodity, it's a commodity that you purchase. But here we're talking about lives. It's absolutely lives, and in this case, sex.'

To the team, the only logical conclusion was to treat the case as they would any other commodity, but instead of buying drugs, for example, they'd be buying sex. When dealing with crime syndicates, these 'buy-and-bust' operations are often the only way for police to prove their criminality in the courts. But pulling off an undercover sting operation is a legal minefield for the cops. In South Africa, the only way for law enforcement officers to do this is through a piece of legislation called section 252A of the Criminal Procedure Act.

'That means we go to the Director of Public Prosecutions and ask for permission to use persons (usually police officers) as agents. We're also asking for a legal pardon (for those persons) because we are then committing a crime, in this case, where we will be paying for sex.'

Police have to tread very carefully here. They are not, by South African law, permitted to use entrapment. As I said, it's tricky legal ground, but in lay terms, a police officer cannot approach you out of the blue on a street corner and offer to sell you drugs. On the other hand, if you had been actively asking for drugs in that area for a while and the police had used an undercover agent to sell to you and then arrest you, it would be another ball game altogether.

'We can use the agent to phone one of the sex workers, to make an appointment, set a time, and of course, then the sex worker must provide the agent with an amount it would cost. We record the whole conversation to use it as evidence later in court.'

Lizelle quickly pointed out that agents are not allowed to take it as far as engaging in sexual activity.

'No sex may take place. Under no circumstances are police or anybody acting as an agent for the police allowed to enter a brothel and have sex with a sex worker. Our evidence at the end of the day will be in the transaction between the agent and the sex worker.'

To further 'bulletproof' their case, the team took it one step further than just the phone calls. They planned to send agents into the brothels during three different 252A operations.

'What we do in these cases is use marked money provided by the state. We borrow X amount from the state, and as soon as the cash is handed over to the sex worker by the agent, the rest of us will pounce.'

Lizelle's team used hidden cameras to record these trans-actions and conducted surveillance nearby when the agents entered. A prearranged signal from the agent let the rest of the team know when to enter and make the arrests. Every single banknote handed over to the sex worker had been meticulously photocopied and noted beforehand, including its unique serial number. The purpose is to prove the crime in court, but also to let investigators follow the money trail.

'So we look at who handles the money, who has possession of the money. In some cases, the money is shared. A small piece goes to the sex worker, another person at the premises might be found with the rest. This can give you a better idea of who plays a management role in the brothel.'

Thomas Hardy once wrote: 'And yet to every bad, there is a worse.' During the first 252A operation, the Hawks uncovered a darker side to Shantel's business. Back in the old SARS building where Lizelle had been taking me through the case, there was an evident change in her demeanour when she got to this part of the story. She'd removed her glasses, and those eyes offered an emerald-tinted glimpse into the pain, suffering and sorrow they'd observed over the years.

'We realised Shantel employed minor children,' she said with an almost imperceptible shudder. 'Obviously, our very first priority is to remove minors from the situation as soon as possible.'

The minor girls were sex workers, sometimes seeing up to ten customers in a day. One sixteen-year-old, who we'll call Melissa to protect her identity, would eventually provide crucial evidence about, and insight into, the horrible conditions they endured.

'During our first 252A operation, we used the opportunity to bring in all the persons we found at the premises,' Lizelle continued. And that included any minors. The police took extra care to assist them, Lizelle said: 'They were removed from those circumstances and made to feel at ease. A victim doesn't belong in the cells, so they were treated with dignity and given the opportunity to really speak to us. And those who were willing to be helped at that time were immediately assisted. They were placed in safe houses run by NGOs in the Cape who we work with very closely.'

Those who were willing to be helped. Read that again: why would they not be? It's an interesting question that lies at the heart of many sex trafficking cases. To answer it, you need to understand human trafficking and the despicable criminals behind it.

According to the US Department of State, there are an estimated 27,6 million trafficking victims worldwide at any given time. In a 2009 global report on trafficking in persons, the United Nations Office on Drugs and Crime (UNODC) found the most common form of human trafficking (79%) to be sexual exploitation. The second most common form (18%) was forced labour. It also found that 20% of victims worldwide were children, although that number was much higher in some parts of Africa and the Mekong region. In parts of West Africa, for example, 100% of the victims were found to be children.

South African cases are notoriously under-reported, and the numbers vary depending on who you speak to. During a briefing to parliament in 2021, police minister Bheki Cele said that between 2018 and 2021, 781 South African children fell victim to child trafficking. But speak to any of the NGOs who work on trafficking cases inside the country on a daily basis, and they'll tell you those numbers are just the tip of the iceberg.

When I was still finding my feet as an investigative journalist, I had a preconceived and rather naive idea about what human trafficking was, perhaps influenced by the seemingly never-ending list of crime dramas and fictionalised Hollywood films on the subject. In my mind's eye, I pictured innocent young women from perfectly suburban homes kidnapped off the streets by gangs of masked men in nondescript black vans. And how those same victims were forced into shipping containers before being sold into slavery, frequently into the harem of some perverted criminal mastermind intent on taking over the world.

But I soon learnt that, in reality, these cases were often far more nuanced, even though the devastating consequences for the victims remained the same. Human trafficking syndicates are just another form of organised crime. And the motivation behind any organised crime is always the same – greed. Criminal enterprises are founded to make money. And the people behind them don't care how they do it.

But if hundreds of young women from decent middle- and upper-class homes suddenly got kidnapped off the streets of major cities every other week, the fallout, public outcry and resulting law enforcement response would be immense. It would put a lot of heat on the traffickers. And that kind of heat would be bad for business. So, how do they do it?

The name of the game is exploitation. And it's much more deviously planned and executed than you might think. Incompetent people do not run successful criminal syndicates. Traffickers, especially, have mastered the art of exploiting their victims. In most cases, the young men and women who fall victim to traffickers are especially vulnerable to the predators. And to the trained criminal eye, they stick out like a sore thumb.

If you were the trafficker, who would be the easier target? A young girl from a wealthy background and stable family life who is the head prefect at a reputable school, or the young girl who has run away from home, been the victim of domestic violence, turned to drugs to deal with her sorrow, and is struggling to survive on the streets?

It's a no-brainer. Victim number one would scream blue murder, perhaps put up a fight. Her parents would pressure law enforcement to find her, and the media would get involved. It would cause a shitstorm for the traffickers. Victim number two may willingly accept the offer of a place to call home, access to drugs and alcohol, and the relative safety of having pimps and security to 'protect' her.

Unfortunately for victim number two, it's too late by the time she realises she's jumped from the proverbial frying pan straight into the fire. She's hooked on the drugs, she needs the traffickers to keep supplying her. She's committed crimes; they could have her locked up, and they know people in the police. And if those aren't enough reasons to stay, the real threat of brutal violence is never far away.

I once met a young sex worker who was so addicted to crack cocaine she wasn't even asking her pimp for her share of the money she earned any more. She'd come from a good home, but unfortunately, at the age of sixteen, she'd fallen in with the wrong crowd and soon became addicted to a variety of illegal drugs. The drug use had inevitably led to clashes with her parents, whom she'd eventually written off. By the time I met her while investigating several brothels in the Pretoria (now known as Tshwane) area, she was so addicted she refused to work or even get out of bed unless she got a 'rock' (one of the street names for crack cocaine, named after its appearance) with which to start her day.

Her parents eventually paid an ex-policeman turned private investigator (PI) to rescue her from the clutches of the trafficking syndicate. The Nigerian men running the brothel she was stuck in were notoriously dangerous and heavy-handed with the women in their employ. The PI managed to get her out, and her parents spent thousands on getting her professional counselling and into drug rehab. Unfortunately, less than a month into treatment, she ran away and returned to the syndicate.

I don't know what became of her, but it is a tragic example of just how drugs can influence a person's life. This is something most people have a hard time comprehending. But I can promise you, addiction, especially to hardcore drugs, is not something to take lightly.

Speak to any drug counsellor, and they'll tell you that two things could happen once an addict hits rock bottom. It could finally become the moment they realise they need to seek help, or be the final stop along the train track that will inevitably lead to prison or death.

I once covered a story about what may be the lowest of the lows in drug culture, a world already so bleak it's hard to imagine anything worse. The story was about a phenomenon called Bluetoothing.

While researching how police were losing the fight against heroin dealers in the Rosettenville area, south of the Johannesburg CBD, I met two addicts we'll call Matthew and Mark. Both men had severe heroin addictions. They were unemployed, homeless, and earning a living by begging for cash from motorists at street corners.

I'd hoped they might turn out to be useful sources. We were looking for the locations of the biggest dealers in the area. During the conversation with them, I'd asked Mark what they did when they didn't have the money to score a hit.

'We Bluetooth,' he'd answered, as if it were the most common thing on earth. I consider myself well-versed in the often-changing landscape of illegal drug lingo, but I'd never heard of Bluetooth before.

'Come with us, we'll show you,' Matthew said. It turned out that's what they were on their way to do when we'd stumbled upon them. I could see the severity of both men's addiction. Honestly, I'd never seen two humans closer to death and still breathing.

We accompanied them to a deserted alleyway nearby. While they made themselves comfortable on the grimy floor, covered in all manner of foul-smelling garbage, they produced the paraphernalia that's the stock in trade of most heroin mainliners: an elastic band used as a tourniquet just above the elbow; a spoon in which the brown heroin powder would be heated up to form a liquid; a lighter to do the heating up; and what was, in this case, quite possibly the world's most used-looking hypodermic syringe and needle.

Mark went through the process, explaining that the duo hadn't made much money in the last few days.

'So we don't even have enough here for one hit,' he said, sucking up the liquid heroin through a needle that looked like it might contain diseases yet to be discovered by medical science. 'This little bit is all I could get,' he mumbled, the elastic band pulled tight in his mouth as the needle sunk into his vein. After injecting the drug, his whole body relaxed in a contented sigh.

Matthew was growing increasingly anxious and mumbled something along the lines of, 'Now it's my turn,' to his partner.

But Mark had just injected the only bit of heroin the two had between them; how would Matthew get his fix? What happened next gives me goosebumps to this day.

Mark took the needle he'd just used, stuck it back into his arm and pulled on the plunger. The vial soon filled up with his own blood. And that's when it hit me, a dawning realisation of what Bluetoothing was all about.

Without a word, he passed the needle to Matthew, who promptly stuck it into his forearm and injected himself with Mark's blood.

Hundreds of questions flooded my mind. How safe was this? Hadn't they heard about HIV? Surely it couldn't possibly give Matthew the same satisfaction? But in the end, I just sat there in horrified silence, filled with both macabre curiosity and an overwhelming sense of pity for the two men who had long ago given up on any hopes of recovery.

It turned out they believed that sharing the blood of an addict who'd just taken a hit of heroin could get the next person high.

'But it's not the same. It just takes the edge off,' Matthew said. 'Just enough to let me hustle for a while.'

Both men were so addicted that they struggled to get up in the mornings without a hit. We offered to get them help, to see if we could find them a spot in a drug rehab centre that wouldn't cost them a cent. But they refused. They'd tried, they said. Rehab wasn't for them.

Traffickers know very well just how binding the chains of drug addiction can be. And they know that, once their victims are hooked, they're just as helpless to escape their fate as Matthew and Mark had been. That's the true exploitation in so many of these cases, and the traffickers have honed it to perfection.

In Cape Town, the 252A operations had the desired effect of providing the Hawks with all the evidence they would need to take on Reyneke-Bridger and her gang. Victims like sixteen-year-old Melissa provided much-needed insight into the syndicate's operations. They described the terrible conditions the sex workers lived in. And although Reyneke-Bridger and her associates were rolling in the dough, the money wasn't spent on food, luxury accommodation or expensive cars. Conditions inside the brothels and the home the masterminds were living in were squalid.

Cellphones confiscated during the raids contained video evidence of the violence many sex workers faced if they got out of line. Lizelle described some of the abhorrent scenes to me.

'We found videos of girls being assaulted, disciplined, tied up with rope. We could follow up information at hospitals, where we found their patient records showing broken arms and stitches. So it exposed this whole other world of what was happening between four walls.'

In most cases, brothels all over the world make use of 'body-guards' or 'heavies'. These are usually physically strong and violent men who keep operations running smoothly under their iron fists. If any of the johns get out of line, they quickly learn the painful error of their ways. This isn't some altruistic endeavour to protect sex workers from harm. It's simply the bosses looking after their investments.

In the Project Madame case, they were, more often than not, employed to keep the sex workers in line. Lizelle's team found video evidence of Melissa being 'disciplined' by one such man, Fareez Allie. Allie's job was a study in contrasts. To the sex workers he was both guardian angel and brutal enforcer. He made sure they obeyed Shantel's rules with an iron fist, but also protected her merchandise from clients who sometimes turned violent.

'His big role was, of course, to also put the fear of God into the sex workers. He was a large, strong man. And if we look at this case where minor children were involved, the fear they had for him was indescribable,' Lizelle recalled.

'And he showed them absolutely no mercy. We saw a video where he disciplined two young women who went out without permission. And he was told by Shantel to assault them. We played this video in court. And the worst of all, and it will stay with me forever, is that he laughed. And he said to his lawyer that it was just a joke.'

One of the victims in the footage was Melissa. Reliving the evidence in court, the video so profoundly affected her that the judge called for an adjournment.

Lizelle remembers the scene clearly. 'She said, looking back at that moment, she recalled the absolute fear she felt. And she felt anger, anger at herself for allowing it to happen. And he slapped those two young girls in their faces with the force that would have jolted a large man. And that was his job. That's what he was paid for . . .'

The young women faced Shantel's unique form of 'discipline' for various reasons, many of which were trivial. Arriving late for an appointment with a john, if the client wasn't satisfied with the service, if they didn't want to participate in the syndicate's other criminal activities. Shantel often waited outside department stores when she sent the women in to steal items such as clothing and perfumes.

'She then sold these items afterwards. It's just another way of making money. At the end of the day, everything was about money for Shantel,' Lizelle said.

Violence wasn't the only way Shantel kept her victims in her vice-like grips. Another common denominator in trafficking cases is what is known to law enforcement officials as debt bondage. Lizelle offered me the perfect explanation.

'If a transgression didn't warrant an assault, according to the syndicate, they paid fines. This later played a huge role in proving the human trafficking element in court. Because the women were placed into debt bondage, they found themselves in so much debt that they had no choice but to stay in the syndicate.'

At the end of the day, it's all about control over the victims. When a sex worker would earn R1 500 per hour, R1 000 would go to the madame. The sex worker could keep R500 – but the moment the fines would come into play, she would earn next to nothing.

'At the end of the day, these girls are doing sessions for free, time and time and time again. We looked at several ledgers and books kept by the syndicate, and you could page through those and see where the girls had made notes like this is a fine, I have to pay this back,' Lizelle said.

The documents showed that the women were forced to work seven days a week, at all hours, seeing between four and thirteen clients daily.

'To think that you're not earning a single cent for it, that's the best example that I can give you about what debt bondage is, and it played a huge role in this case.'

After three successful 252A operations, Lizelle and her team were ready to pounce.

'We set a date to terminate the project, which happened on a large scale. We brought in other units, some of them from other provinces, and in one night, we did a massive take-down operation. We had arrest warrants for all the accused, all the addresses, and we managed to arrest them all.'

After the arrests, the Hawks discovered vast sums of money going through Shantel's bank accounts. She dispersed the funds to several of her accomplices. Even her son was eventually arrested after a forensic investigation revealed his account had also received much of the funds. Money laundering charges were also added to the case. It was also during this deep dive into the gang's finances that the Hawks came across Mr X, the man who had been extorted for millions after he had visited one of Shantel's brothels.

This same forensic analysis gave investigators a surprising insight into where Shantel and her crew's money was going.

'If one looks at the conditions they were living in, even more so the sex workers, it was squalid. The fridges were empty. The places were incredibly dirty. They never cleaned. Hygiene was not high on their list of priorities. And they got by with the absolute minimum. Then you can't help but wonder, with all their millions, where is the luxury, where is the abundance, where is the car and the mansion?'

Lizelle and her team were astonished to discover the answer: casinos.

'We realised that Shantel, Juan Warren and Norman Bridger had severe gambling problems. We pulled their records at some of the Cape casinos and found that she'd lost more than a million rand at just one of the venues. That was just what we could find on paper at the time. So this was a lady who managed a human trafficking brothel, who assaulted and exploited her victims, who made them live with almost no food or clothes, but was quite happy to throw away a million rand at the casino.'

After their arrests and faced with the overwhelming evidence gathered by the investigating team, Shantel, Juan and Norman entered into plea deals with the state. They were each sentenced to twenty years behind bars on charges ranging from racketeering, money laundering and kidnapping of a minor to trafficking in persons for sexual purposes.

'Shantel was undoubtedly the brains behind the operation, and if you listened to the evidence, people lived in fear of the power she wielded. But all three got twenty years in prison, which is where they belong,' Lizelle added.

Shantel's son was found guilty of participating in an organised crime enterprise and living on the proceeds of prostitution, among others. To the investigating team's disappointment, Fareez Allie received only a three-year sentence for the assault charges. Other syndicate members, including sex workers who had participated in the trafficking operations, were also charged and found guilty of money laundering, racketeering and kidnapping of a minor, among other things.

Lizelle took me through the court case and resulting sentences with stern-faced pride, and rightfully so, since this was the first time in South African history that members of a syndicate had been found guilty of human trafficking under the Prevention of Organised Crime Act. But those steely green eyes turned soft (accompanied by a smile about a mile wide) when I asked her what had become of Melissa, the sixteen-year-old caught in the vicious web of deceit spun by Shantel and her associates.

'Today, she is a nursery school teacher. She turned her back on her past. It wasn't an easy thing for her to do. She had the support of one of her family members, but her drug addiction was still a problem. Today, she's completely clean, she doesn't use drugs any more. She changed her life completely, and it's going very well with her.'

Lizelle stayed in touch with Melissa, and although she's humble about her work, to me it's one of her most endearing qualities, one we need more of in our police force. Before leaving her offices, I shared a last cup of coffee with her in a deserted area of the old building, a large open-plan space where several run-down-looking windows offered a rather solemn view of the dreary Cape weather.

'The day you work a trafficking case, it is not something that you do today and tomorrow the case is over. You walk a road, you walk a road with these people, for as long as they might need you, you're there for them.'

It's a road I could tell had taken its toll on Captain Lizelle Herbst. She's seen horrors that you and I can only imagine. But standing there watching the raindrops gather on the worn glass panes, sipping from a fearsomely strong but all too welcome cup of coffee, I had the feeling it's not a road she's done travelling yet.

'Sometimes I wonder how some of these victims are still standing after what they've been through. These are circumstances me and you can't fathom. We've never gone to bed hungry; we've never gone to bed in absolute terror. Our bodies have never been repeatedly abused. We don't carry those scars. The things these people go through are a reality. And the faster we realise that it is a reality and start doing something about it, the faster we can get them out of those circumstances. Human trafficking, especially human trafficking involving minors, is something that breaks a person's heart. We can all be grateful that we have someone to fall back on, those of us who have someone who is a rock, a foundation. These people have nothing.'

2

THE FOREX HEISTS

165 Meyer Street, Germiston, is a tall building just a few minutes' walk from the Germiston Magistrate's Court and the local police station. Finding parking in the city's crowded CBD took me nearly ten minutes. And once I did, it was a rather tight fit.

Meyer Street has seen better days, like many of our inner-city areas. I'd nearly caused a minor traffic incident by swerving for the mother of all potholes on my way up the street. As a reward for my advanced driving skills, a taxi driver, whose open windows were blaring a base beat so loudly that I wondered if it might set off the surrounding car alarms, flipped me the bird.

A lot of people get upset about our inner-city decay. Perhaps rightfully so. But it's a problem you'll find in any city, anywhere in the world. I found a uniquely South African vibe among the faded to-let signs, the nightclubs that doubled as guesthouses, and the street merchants manning makeshift stalls. A pulse that beat deeper than any taxi's set of subwoofers.

Away from the hustle and bustle of the street outside, I'd passed through security and entered the lift, hitting the button to take me to the twelfth floor of the Hawks' offices. A reedy, metallic-sounding voice warned me that the lift doors were about to close. Not sure if I was to be thankful for this useless bit of information, I couldn't help wondering when the last time the lift had been serviced. I take my hat off to the thousands of government employees who have to use similar lifts every day. They don't inspire much confidence.

Having emerged safely at my destination, I was met by a large steel security gate, which seemed to be accessed with a biometric scanner. You might be able to get into the offices unannounced, but it would be a mission.

Before I could ring the little blue doorbell mounted next to the scanner, I heard a deep voice booming down the corridor behind the gate. This is the voice of a man who enjoys life, I thought. It was loud but jovial and rambunctious. It sounded like he was greeting colleagues as he passed their offices, engaging in the kind of banter typical among co-workers who know each other well. Before he arrived at the gate, I felt that the owner of that voice could turn out to be Lt Col Masenxani Chauke, the man I'd come here to see.

And although we'd never met, when he rounded the corner and glanced at me, he must have had a similar thought.

'Ahh, Mr Coetzer?' He asked with a big grin that touched the corners of his dark-brown eyes. 'Come in, come in. We'll be sitting in the boardroom, first door on your left. Let me go and fetch the docket.'

The lieutenant colonel cut an imposing figure. Along with his deep baritone voice and dark, bushy moustache, his tall frame was dressed in black trousers and a checked shirt, long sleeves rolled up to his elbows. He looked competent and capable, the qualities you need to rise through the ranks in the DPCI's National Prevention Against Violent Crimes (NPVC) unit.

Like so many of his counterparts, he doesn't trust journalists. And he's not keen on the spotlight. In that sense, he's an old-school copper. They're wary of the media. Before I'd finally met him, it had taken some convincing to let me tell his story, even though I had written approval from head office.

But as we went through his files, all that was soon forgotten as we got into the nuts and bolts of the case.

It had started more than a decade ago. Between 2012 and 2014, Gauteng and its surrounding provinces had been hit by violent bank robberies.

'In those two years,' Masenxani told me, '25 bank robberies were committed that had a similar MO. The targets were all smaller banks that dealt in forex. It is the kind of place you visit to exchange your rand for dollars before an overseas trip. Places like Travelex, Bidvest, Eurodollar.'

Gideon Jones spent decades in the police force before entering the private sector as a forensic investigator. He was an excellent detective before being promoted to the head of the Undercover Division of the Organised Crime Unit's Intelligence wing. He is a close friend of mine, and his wealth of operational experience in the SAPS meant that he was an invaluable asset during my research of this book. 'Most bank robberies in South Africa follow a typical pattern,' Gideon told me. 'You usually have a group of suspects who enter the bank. Some will have to overpower security, while the rest get to the tellers. They'll be armed and use violence to get what they came for. That's almost always the case.'

Masenxani said these banks made for easy targets. They were physically smaller premises than most commercial banks, which meant they were easier for criminals to control. They didn't have much by way of security. And because of the nature of their business, they always had cash.

'These guys were busy; on one day, they hit five different banks in Gauteng,' Masenxani told me. The gang's MO was simple yet effective. 'It was the same thing in most of the cases. Men came in and would pretend to be customers. They were well dressed, and they looked like clients.'

A lookout was posted just outside the entrance doors to keep an eye out for any signs of trouble. Inside, the robbers would produce 9mm pistols and overpower the bank's employees. The security guards were the first to be targeted. Once they'd been subdued at gunpoint, the rest of the gang would break open the secure doors meant to protect the tellers.

'They used a crowbar, and if you watch the footage, it didn't take them long to get in,' Masenxani said. He later took me through some of the CCTV footage that the different banks' cameras had captured. It was astounding to see supposedly high-tech security doors broken open in seconds with something as outdated as a crowbar.

'Once in, they overpowered the tellers. Many of them were females. These ladies had guns shoved into their faces. The robbers would come in and just scream at them, open, open! If they didn't cooperate, they were beaten with the firearms.'

It was a terrifying ordeal for the tellers. The robbers were brutally efficient, getting them to empty their cash registers and forcing them to open the safes in the back. Like most CCTV footage, the scenes in the banks had no audio. But watching the panicked faces of the tellers during the robberies, how they were manhandled at gunpoint, and the states of shock they were left in afterwards was somehow made all the more compelling by the lack of sound. In most of the cases, the robbers were in and out of the banks in under five minutes.

'The gang didn't always use the same people during the robberies,' Masenxani told me. 'But in all the cases, one man was always present. He was the first guy to enter the banks, and he was the first to produce his pistol. It was clear from the outset that he was the leader. Later on, we identified him as Sikhumbuzo Sibanda.'

At the time, investigators had yet to discover that Sibanda, a Zimbabwean national, had a long history of run-ins with the law.

'He had been previously arrested and convicted for possessing an unlicensed firearm and armed robbery. But at that time, he was using the alias David Ndlovu,' the lieutenant colonel told me, pointing to a mugshot of Sibanda in his files. The middle-aged Sibanda seemed unassuming, just your everyday man on the street. Even while watching the moments leading up to the robberies captured on CCTV, you'd be hard put to guess he was the leader of a ruthless gang of robbers.

But he was. As David Ndlovu, Sibanda had served his sentence before being deported back to Zimbabwe. In the intervening years, he'd somehow re-entered the country as Sikhumbuzo Sibanda. Unfortunately, as a country we are all too well known for our porous borders.

'He looked like a nice guy; even when I eventually questioned him, he was respectful and calm. But when he went into those banks, his behaviour changed. Completely. But if he were sitting across from you and talking to you, you wouldn't believe this guy was a criminal.'

This is another one of the dichotomies I've encountered most in my work as an investigative journalist. For whatever reason, we all seem to think criminals will look or act a certain way. We can't describe what they would look like or how they would act, but we expect something different from what we are. I've met quite a few hardened criminals in my career. Good journalists have sources in high and low places, after all. With only a few exceptions, criminals are just ordinary people. They often have spouses and children, just like me or you. They wear the same clothes as us, drive the same cars and send their kids to the same (if not better) schools. Many of them are religious, and they'll sit right next to you in church. Outside their life of crime, they face all the same little challenges we do. They also have to pay bills and worry about an elderly parent. They are also diagnosed with deadly diseases.

And yet, deep down inside, we expect them to look different. Act differently. Perhaps there is some deeply ingrained need for us to believe that the monsters among us would stand out and be easily recognisable.

But nothing could be further from the truth. Life isn't that black-and-white, no matter how much we want it to be. Think of any documentary you've ever seen about a serial killer, for instance. How often do you hear interviewees say something along the lines of, 'He looked like any other guy. He was kind and gentle . . . '

At the height of Sibanda's crime spree, the Hawks hadn't yet been called on to look into the cases. One of the problems was that they had all been reported at different police stations in different precincts. No one had put two and two together yet.

That was until SABRIC came into the picture. The South African Banking Risk Information Centre is a non-profit company formed by South Africa's major banks. Their job is to assist the industry in combatting organised crime-related risks. SABRIC thoroughly analysed the crimes, going through all of the CCTV footage. And they realised that they were all probably the work of the same gang.

'They approached some of my seniors in the Hawks to look at the cases,' Masenxani told me. 'General Sibiya then put together a task team to investigate the cases. And I became the investigating officer on the case.'

The team consolidated all the dockets and started re-evaluating the crimes. Masenxani knew they'd have to act fast; Sibanda's crew had become increasingly violent.

'At one of the heists in Fordsburg, a security guard was shot. As well as an innocent bystander.'

They both survived, but it clearly indicated that Sibanda wouldn't hesitate to use violent means to get at the cash.

'In these kinds of crimes,' Gideon said, 'the robbers have to move fast. They have to enter quickly, and they have to overpower their opposition as soon as possible. They have to stamp their authority on the security and the employees. And they'll often use violence.'

The gang wanted to be in and out of the premises as quickly as possible.

'They'll hit people, kick them. They'll count on the employees to cooperate when confronted with violence. There aren't many people who don't cooperate when they have a firearm pressed against their heads. But it's all about fear. They need to instil fear into the employees. And through the fear, they gain control.'

But when the robbers encountered opposition, things turned deadly.

'In the Fordsburg case, they were accosted by a security guard outside the bank, and a shooting ensued. And it shows you just how dangerous these situations can become – an innocent member of the public nearly lost their life in the crossfire.'

In February 2014, shortly after the Hawks had taken over the case, Masenxani had a breakthrough.

'While we were gathering evidence in Gauteng,' he said, 'our Crime Intelligence teams in KZN got information that a group of robbers were headed to a shopping mall to commit an armed robbery.' The information was passed on to local police, who could stop the vehicles the robbers were travelling in and arrest the suspects. 'This was in Empangeni, near Richards Bay. They were on their way to rob a Pick n Pay, but they were intercepted before they got there. And after their arrests, Crime Intelligence in central Johannesburg were informed.'

The information was filtered through to the DPCI's bank robbery task team.

'The information was that the suspects were from Gauteng. And I wondered if these weren't the same guys. So, I went down to KZN,' Masenxani said.

He travelled to Empangeni, accompanied by some of the task team's members, to verify the information. Once there, he was convinced these were the same men he was after.

'I returned to Gauteng and arranged for a massive ID parade.'

It was a logistical nightmare. Permission had to be obtained from the Department of Correctional Services to move the ten suspects arrested in KZN to Gauteng. Witnesses, most of whom had been the victims inside the banks during the robberies, had to be asked to avail themselves. Remember, this was from 25 cases that had occurred over two years.

'We tracked them down, and luckily many people agreed to participate in the ID parade.'

Identity parades in South Africa are not all that dissimilar from what you might have seen in a movie or television series. Gideon has attended more than just a few. 'The parade will be handled by an independent police official, not the investigating officer,' he told me. 'That's to prevent the criminals from having any opportunity to use anything against the police during trial. The witness will be called in, and they will be asked to look through a two-way mirror at a row of people who will be lined up against the wall.'

Some of those people will be the suspects, and others will be members of the public or even police officers who have never met the witness. The proceedings have to be seen to be exceedingly fair. 'It's really important that there are no issues in court later. So, for instance, there may not be any interaction between the investigating officer and the witness at the parade. He can't say look at number three or look at number eight.'

Special attention is also given to the people lined up beside the suspects. They must be broadly of the same race, gender and age as the suspects.

'Then, the witness will be asked to identify the suspects they had seen on a specific day, committing a specific crime. And the witness must choose correctly for the ID parade to succeed.'

ID parades like these are not always as successful as you might think. Many witnesses have gone through extreme trauma during the events. Years might pass before they're called upon to identify the perpetrators. The criminals themselves might have changed their appearances drastically. Someone might have grown a beard or lost weight since the crime.

This is something I've experienced myself, over and over, while working on my own stories. I've often met the subject of an undercover investigation while carrying a hidden camera or audio recording device, hoping to use the evidence to expose them. I'd usually have a very good description of the person and, in many cases, a photograph or two. But it's a lot harder than you may think to identify someone you've only seen in a photograph in real life. A close-up of someone's face, for instance, will not tell you how tall that person is, how they're built, how they walk and talk.

I was surprised that any of the witnesses in this case could identify the robbers. The attacks happened so fast, they were constantly threatened with guns, and they were under extreme pressure. Luckily, quite a few of Sibanda's gang were positively identified.

The evidence was enough to charge Sibanda and his men and place them on the court roll. They applied for bail, but Masenxani was able to oppose the applications in court. Many of the men had previous convictions for similar crimes, and it was clear from their actions during the robberies that they posed a risk to society.

But the Hawks' task team wanted to build a bulletproof case for the upcoming trial. So Masenxani decided to take things one step further.

'I went to every bank and downloaded the CCTV footage. I had an expert from our cyber unit accompany me, and he did the downloads. This was so we could tell the court we had original copies of the material and that the chain of custody could not be questioned.'

The chain of custody is one of those police terms the public doesn't often get to hear, but is one of the most critical elements of the job. To be presented with a broken chain of custody is every defence attorney's dream come true. It's often what's gone wrong behind the scenes when you hear that someone 'got off on a technicality'.

The term refers to the process of gathering and documenting evidence and the order in which that evidence was handled during the investigation. Each bit of evidence gathered by police needs to be recorded, sealed in evidence bags and marked with unique identifiers. Every person who handled the evidence needs to be meticulously documented. It's the only way a court will accept the evidence during a trial.

The OJ Simpson trial is perhaps one of the best-documented examples of how a broken chain of custody can influence a case. Simpson's attorneys managed to cast doubt on crucial blood evidence during the trial. They could prove that blood samples taken at the crime scene had been handled by multiple officers at various times during the investigation. Critically, those officers had not been noted on the Chain of Custody form. This allowed the defence team to create doubt in the jurors' minds by implying that the evidence may have been planted to make Simpson appear guilty.

Masenxani transferred the footage to the Krugersdorp branch of the Local Criminal Records Centre (LCRC) for facial comparison analysis. There are 92 of these located throughout South Africa. LCRC staff are responsible for collecting, managing and safely storing evidence from crime scenes.

'We typically work in the field,' Capt. Corné de Bod told me. 'We gather evidence at crime scenes, like fingerprints, blood or DNA evidence. And then we analyse the evidence to see if suspects can be tied to crime scenes in that way.'

After some effort – the Hawks and the SAPS are technically one organisation, but the Hawks couldn't give me the green light to speak to Corné, which had to be obtained from her provincial head in the SAPS – I managed to get permission to interview the West Rand-based forensic investigator.

Corné is the woman who analysed the CCTV footage, and she was asked to do facial comparisons on the men in the Hawks' custody. Her office, like the woman herself, was a study in contrasts. It was one of the few police offices I'd been in that had been decorated with brightly coloured personal items and had a relaxed and friendly atmosphere.

The captain was the kind of person you'd expect to be the first neighbour to bring a tray of cookies over if you moved into a new house. Warm, friendly and sincere, she wore a bright-pink shirt and matching flower-print jacket on the day we met.

As we sat down to a cup of coffee she'd brewed on a little gas stove setup in the corner of her office – her load-shedding combat kit, she'd remarked – I noticed one of the few clues to the grisly nature of her work prominently displayed on her desk.

Mounted on a wooden display stand were the models of two human skulls, one complete with plastic eyes that seemed to add a morbid quality to the display. Before we got into her story, I couldn't resist asking her how she'd got into this line of work. 'I've always been fascinated by science,' she told me. 'And yes, you're right, I have to walk into some horrific crime scenes. Some of the worst are when children have been murdered. But that's when I remind myself I'm here to speak for that victim. They can't do that any more, but the evidence I find on a scene might lead me to that person's killer. And that's what I focus on.'

A pathologist who worked at Forensic Pathology Services in Hillbrow had once told me something similar about performing autopsies on victims of violent crime. I'd been allowed a behind-the-scenes look at her work as part of a profile piece I'd been tasked to compile on the state's forensic pathologist just before the infamous Oscar Pistorius trial began.

That particular experience is not one I'll easily forget. Situated about a block away from the Constitutional Court in Johannesburg, the Medico-Legal Laboratory is a squat double-storey building, its dozens of street-facing windows covered in bland steel bars and security meshing. From the outside, it looks every bit like a prison building.

But it's only once you get inside that the gravity of the work done there really sinks in. The first thing that hits you is the smell. The scent that fills the offices and hallways is the unmistakable smell of death. It cloys the air, so thick you could cut it with a knife.

Our team had been permitted to film the areas where the bodies were kept and autopsied. But before entering, we were asked to put on personal protective equipment, or PPE. Any thoughts about whether that would be necessary were quickly banished when we were asked not to touch any surfaces. We could pick up blood-borne diseases, we were warned – hepatitis, for example, or even HIV.

The cutting floor, as it was called, was a large open hall and, like so many government institutions, in need of a decent lick of paint. This was the area where autopsies were performed. I'd been expecting a small room, perhaps an operating theatre.

But in reality, the cutting floor had four bays so that four pathologists could work on four bodies at once. They are so busy that having only four autopsies to complete in a single day would be considered a slow morning. Most of the bodies, we were told, were the victims of violent crimes.

Later, we were shown the fridges where the bodies were stored. We had to step carefully as the passageway leading to them had pools of blood on the floor, where two newly arrived corpses were lying on steel stretchers. Again, and rather naively, I'd expected to see the small stainless-steel drawers you often see in the movies. The ones that open so that a single person can be rolled out on a sliding table. But these were large, walk-in fridges that held many bodies. The light in the one they opened for us wasn't working.

It was perhaps the most macabre experience of my career – not one I'd recommend to anyone with a sensitive disposition. But it's also given me the utmost respect for the people who have made a career working in forensics. The kinds of dedicated men and women who will investigate brutal murder scenes or examine horrifically dismembered bodies to provide answers and hopefully justice to bereaved family members.

Corné had an album of photographs of Sibanda's crew, taken after their arrests, compiled to perform her facial analysis.

'So it was my job to compare those control photos of the suspects with the footage from the banks.' It's a tricky process – much of the footage was simply of such bad quality that comparisons couldn't be successfully performed. 'But in this case, I could positively identify seven of the suspects, linking them to the bank robberies.'

She took me through the facial recognition process, which she performed using digital software. 'We start by identifying the morphological landmarks on a person's face. These land-marks are the person's eyes, the nose, the lips, and the shape of their face. The eyebrows . . . ' Other landmarks include moles or scars. 'Those are the kinds of features of a person's face that won't ever really change. They might age, but they'll always stay the same. Scars are the same, they are unique, and they never really change.'

Investigators like Corné then use those landmarks to see if they can be found on the people in the CCTV footage.

'If a person wants to, for example, shave off their beard, it won't help. The shape of that beard and how the hair will grow back will always stay the same.'

Interestingly, in South African law, for fingerprints to be positively matched, forensic investigators have to find and point out a specific number of similarities. That's not the case with facial comparisons.

'With fingerprints, you must be able to point out at least seven different features with no difference. In facial com-parisons, a qualified forensic investigator can go to court with even one point, such as a unique scar. And they can testify to it. But obviously the more you find, the better the chances of the judge accepting your testimony,' Corné said.

Gideon says for an investigating officer, there's no such thing as too much evidence.

'What that person always tries and does, in fact, what they always have to do, is to gather as much evidence in a case as possible. There is never really a time when you can say I have enough evidence.' He's had cases where suspects plead guilty, only to change their pleas later. 'And that's why you can't stop the investigation because someone pleads guilty. If you have fingerprints, DNA or even video footage, you must gather all the evidence and have it forensically analysed.'

'That was really strong evidence in court,' Masenxani told me, referring to Corné's work. 'They couldn't deny that they had been at the robbery. We had experts who testified that the people on the footage were the people in court.'

The court case turned out to be the biggest part of Masenxani's case, as it often does. The bail hearing alone took months. 'I stood in the dock for about two months to oppose bail,' he said. Most of them had prior convictions, and I was successful.'

The trial got underway in 2016.

'It was a long trial indeed. I called 130 witnesses. They were all cross-examined in the High Court.'

Masenxani said that, for many of the witnesses, especially some of the tellers who had been assaulted during the robberies, it had been a gruelling experience. 'Some of them had been highly traumatised. Some of them broke down during testimony. There were a lot of tears. The court had to adjourn several times to allow them to compose themselves.'

Corné had a lot of sympathy for the witnesses. Even after all her years on the force, she says, she still feels some anxiety testifying in cases. 'You do feel anxious. Some of these guys are hardened criminals. They are big guys, most of them were bigger than me, and they come across as quite domineering.'

The captain's work wasn't done once she'd produced her forensic reports. During the trial, she was required to explain her findings to the court. And in South African courts, unlike what you may have seen on television, she couldn't just point at the accused to identify them to the court.

'I would describe my findings to the court, visually explaining the similarities in landmarks on the photographic and

CCTV exhibits. And then I'd be asked if I saw that person in court, and I would have to walk to that person and identify the landmarks on their face, and confirm to the court that it was indeed the same person.'

Masenxani spent much time with his witnesses during the trial, often reassuring them after they broke down.

'A lot of them were very scared,' he said. 'But I would tell them that their testimony could help put a stop to these people. And they understood that, and they testified.'

Sibanda and his nine fellow accused were charged under the POCA (the Prevention of Organised Crime Act) on racketeering charges, among others. This is a powerful piece of South African criminal legislation designed to deal with organised crime. In short, it allowed the state to charge the gang for armed robberies and running a criminal enterprise.

'It was important because these crimes were organised,' Masenxani said. 'They had meetings, planned the robberies, had targets, and did so repeatedly.'

The state's efforts paid off. In a trial that continued until 2019, eight of the ten accused received double life sentences to be served concurrently. Sibanda, the ringleader, was among those found guilty, Masenxani told me.

'Two of the suspects were acquitted. For the rest, life sentences meant that they would spend 25 years in jail without any parole. Direct imprisonment.'

When I left his office, Lt Col Chauke accompanied me to the ground floor. During the ride down in the lift, with the same metallic voice determinedly warning would-be passengers that the doors were about to close, he shared his final thoughts on the case.

'It's a dangerous country, and it's become more dangerous since I started the job. These guys carry high-calibre weapons, aren't afraid to use them and shoot indiscriminately in public places. They want to achieve what they want to achieve,' he mused, hands in his pockets. 'We need to be dedicated if we want to win the war. When duty calls, we have to respond.'

That's a sentiment I'm sure many of us can agree with.

3

THE HITMAN,
THE AVOCADOS AND
THE GREEDY WIFE

Extracts from the SAPS transcription, translated from the original Afrikaans.

Voice File Number: White River CAS126/03/2017
– [Video File]
Audio Length: 03:31
Number of Pages: 5
Date of Transcript: 12-07-2017

PAGE 1
> **Man:** Are you going to stop there?
> **Woman:** Yes, I'm going to stop there I want to get avocados, and a few fruits so . . .
> **Man:** Good, all right then we'll do it there because then it can be done behind those stalls.

PAGE 3

Woman: Okay I'll get in contact with you as soon as the insurance pays out, then I can get cash . . .

Man: How long can it take?

Woman: It should take about a month or two, it doesn't take that long.

Man: Okay.

Woman: Okay, how much?

Man: How much did you think?

Woman: R20 000.

PAGE 4

Man: So that's right, we'll see then, because I've gotten the photo now of him.

Woman: Oh, oh yes.

Man: They sent it to me.

Woman: Oh okay.

Man: Just one shot not two?

Woman: Make it two.

Man: We must be sure he's dead.

Woman: Yes.

It's a conversation that will make the hairs stand up on the back of your neck. Yet the woman so casually discussing the murder of her husband with the hitman she'd hired sounded like she was enjoying herself. Even happy about it.

But to understand this story and the events leading up to this fateful day in 2017, I must take you back to 2013. To a tropical paradise in Mozambique and a small holiday resort on one of that country's gorgeous white sandy beaches. And to the South African man who owned and operated it. A man who was living his lifelong dream . . .

'I was doing something I loved doing, you know, diving and launching, taking people out, looking at reefs and corals, beautiful fish, sharks . . . ' Remembering his previous life in Ponta do Ouro, Mozambique, brings a huge smile to Carlos Ferreira's genial face. The Portuguese-born South African is reminiscing while strolling along a beach in Cape Town, where he now lives. He's dressed in a white golf shirt printed in a palm tree motif. He's rolled up his black denim pants and is carrying a pair of loafers in his hands. His smile is infectious, and you can't help but laugh with him when he laughs.

'I had a small lodge with a couple of rooms that I used to rent out, so ja, life was good,' he said, gazing out at a clear blue sea. With the cool breeze wafting through his steely grey hair, he wouldn't look out of place playing the role of some swashbuckling seafarer in a Netflix series.

The lodge was called Primo Cabanas, and it was a little slice of paradise for the tourists who flocked there, mostly for the diving. Situated on the beach, between palm trees and dense tropical greenery, the brightly decorated rooms and popular bar offered city dwellers the perfect getaway. In 2013, while taking a diving group out on his boat, Carlos first met Maria, the woman who would become his wife.

'So she was one of the divers on the boat,' Carlos said. 'And it looked like she took a liking to me, and I responded, you know. And we hooked up.' After a whirlwind romance, the couple were married later that year. In photos from the time, the red-haired Maria, often called Marietjie by her friends, looks happy and healthy. Their relationship seemed idyllic, and the happy couple could often be found taking their dogs for long walks on the beach or enjoying a few drinks with guests as the sun set over a majestic African coastline. 'Before I met her, I was lonely,' Carlos commented. 'And she was actually very, very sweet, you know.' Little did he know that in the years to come, not only would his life with Maria take on a more sour note, it would turn downright deadly.

Of all the Hawks' officers I've met researching this book, no one quite put me in mind of the legendary British secret agent James Bond as much as Col Danie Hall. Looking into his background, I quickly realised that this was a man with such an exemplary track record in the police that his stories alone would fill volumes.

I'd driven down to the DPCI's Middelburg offices in Mpumalanga to meet him, dodging endless trucks and pothole-filled roads to get to the small mining town. Having parked in front of the typically bland brown brick offices, I was greeted with the sounds of diesel generators humming in the distance. Load shedding.

Although I know that the police have not been exempted from the national power cuts that have devastated the South African economy, it still blows my mind to think that one of our most elite units should be stuck without power for hours on end. Imagine being the investigating officer on a massive fraud case, where the documentary evidence alone takes up a whole van load. How do you prepare for court without electricity when something as simple as sending an email or printing an affidavit becomes an issue?

Walking down an insipid cream-coloured corridor lit only by the beams of afternoon sun casting bright squares of light on a brown-tiled floor, I heard footsteps down a corridor to my right. Dress shoes. Male. Tall.

Since becoming an investigative journalist, I've found taking extra note of your surroundings not only helpful but also essential. I've been threatened by gangsters, drug dealers and notorious underworld characters. I've been told I'd be arrested on trumped-up charges by corrupt policemen. Illegal miners have shot at me. Situational awareness, as those in the know call it, could be a lifesaver. Almost every interview I've ever done with a person who was attacked on a street corner or had their car hijacked as they entered their driveway started with the words, 'They came out of nowhere.'

No, they didn't. They'd been following you, watching you, waiting for the perfect time to pounce. In a country where alarming crime statistics have reached dizzying heights, being aware of your surroundings is one of the simplest and most effective ways of keeping yourself safe. It might sound paranoid, but just because you're paranoid doesn't mean they're not out to get you . . .

So, I've turned what a psychiatrist once called my hyper-vigilance (as if it was a problem I should deal with) into a little game I play in my mind. I do it to while away the lonely hours travelling to see sources or follow up on leads. Listening, observing, analysing. And in this case, I was pleased to see that my guess about the appearance of the owner of those footsteps was spot-on.

Turning the corner, the charismatic Col Hall greeted me with a huge smile and firm handshake, dressed to a tee in a black suit, white dress shirt, mottled red tie and matching pocket square. Immaculately polished dress shoes and neatly trimmed hair rounded off the overall appearance.

As he led the way to the small conference room he'd arranged for us to use, I immediately sensed a man who knew what he was doing. Later on, going through some of his dockets with him, I wasn't surprised to find each one meticulously filed, neatly arranged and colour coded.

When I met Danie in 2022, he was assigned to the DPCI's Anti-Corruption Unit. When Maria Ferreira crossed his path, he'd still been part of the Serious Organised Crime Unit operating from Middelburg.

'In 2017, I got a call from an informant,' he started the story, browsing through a large lever arch file that formed part of the Ferreira case. 'And he informed me that he had information about a woman who lived in Mozambique. And she wanted to have her husband murdered. And that she was very serious about it.'

The woman was Maria Ferreira, who'd met, fallen in love with and married Carlos in Mozambique in 2013. According to the informant, Danie would have to move fast if he wanted to prevent the murder – Maria was planning to get a hitman to take Carlos out during a trip to South Africa that weekend.

'According to the informant, he'd been to the lodge in 2016. And one night, she spontaneously opened up to him around the dinner table. And she asked him to help her murder Carlos's brother. He and his wife were a financial burden to them. And he realised that she was quite serious. And he told her, I can't just murder your husband's brother. She told him that the brother was ill, that he had HIV. And she asked our informant, but how long does it take them to die? And he told her that a person could live quite long with the right medication. And then she said no, but that's too long. She couldn't wait that long.'

The informant told Maria he wouldn't get involved in that kind of thing. And although the conversation had been quite unsettling, he left things there and returned to South Africa. Meanwhile, Carlos had no idea what Maria was up to behind his back. He does recall that their relationship had started taking a turn for the worse just a few months after their whirlwind romance.

'She was drinking heavily,' Carlos told me. 'One day, she was home alone, and I went to buy pizza. She was like, I feel like pizza, you know. And I went out, I waited like an hour for this pizza to come out. Ponta do Ouro sometimes serves a little bit slow . . . So when I came back, she was in a pool of blood.' Carlos said there was blood all over the place. Frightened, he asked Maria what had happened.

'She said no, the border people came here and raped me. And I called the police.' But on arrival, the police couldn't find any signs that anyone else had been near Maria's rooms.

'They said look, we aren't finding any footsteps here. And there's the wallet. Her wallet had like R10 000 in it, but that didn't disappear. And the policeman said I don't think there was anybody here.' A dark cloud crossed his face, recalling this time in their lives. He gazed at the far-off horizon, a thin blue line shimmering in the midday sun. 'That's when I started realising that there's something not right going on.'

Maria later admitted to Carlos that she hadn't been raped. It was the first of many similarly bizarre incidents that would trouble their marriage. Things got worse as her drinking, mixed with prescription medications for depression, resulted in an increasingly toxic mess for Carlos and the residents of Primo Cabanas.

'So I surprised her the one time, and when I walked into the lounge, I startled her. As she stood up, I saw this huge kitchen knife under her, and I thought but what is this now?

Is that for me?' He had every right to be suspicious: Maria had previously told Carlos she was in trouble with the South African authorities and had come to Mozambique to lie low.

'Then you start thinking, you know. She says that she was accused of murdering her late husband. I don't know, it works on your mind, you know.' Maria had told Carlos that she was being falsely accused. I've since discovered that, although she was a person of interest to police in her previous husband's murder, investigators never found enough proof to take the case to court.

According to Carlos, his relationship wasn't the only thing in decline. Maria often went on spending sprees, cleaning out his bank accounts with the ATM card he'd given her. Things got so bad financially that he eventually considered closing the business.

'That's when things really got a bit haywire . . . because the way she was operating, we weren't going anywhere . . . There was no money,' he told me with a wry smile, 'because she'd spent it all.'

Maria even went so far as to scupper a deal between Carlos and a prospective buyer for a part of the lodge.

'She spoilt this whole deal, you know. The guy was horrified because she went and spread bad stories about me. How I supposedly slept with my brother and how I sold drugs on the property. I don't know where she came up with all these things.'

When the deal fell through, Carlos confronted Maria.

'So she acknowledged that she'd spoilt the deal. But she said I'll fix up the deal. And this is how she got me to go to South Africa, to White River.'

Unbeknown to Carlos, Maria had again contacted the same informant who'd approached Danie with the information. In the unit's Middelburg offices, the colonel continued to give me the rundown of his part in the intriguing story.

'In 2017, Maria contacted the informant again. And she said, remember what we spoke of last time? Now I want you to murder Carlos.'

Maria had asked the informant to play the role of a prospective buyer for the lodge. That made it possible for her to convince Carlos to accompany her to White River in South Africa, where the informant lived. The trip was arranged under the auspices of Carlos meeting the buyer. Danie outlined the rest of the plan.

'So the informant told me that Maria was looking for a hitman and that she had asked him to act as a middleman to arrange the hit on Carlos. She went so far as to send him emails, and in the emails, she went as far as saying she'd worked it all out very well. She had a plan A and a plan B.'

Reading through the emails, you're given a chilling account of a woman hellbent on the murder of her husband and the devious lengths she was willing to go to achieve her goals. Maria's email to the informant has been translated from the original Afrikaans. She started by sweetening the deal with the would-be hitman:

As I promised you, if you help me get rid of my problem, I'll give you a place here on my land where you can build yourselves a wooden house, and I'll put it in your name.

I've told Carlos that you're interested in buying a stand here by us for R1.2 million.

[. . .] It's the only way I can get him to drive there to you.

I have two suggestions on how we can solve my problem. Number one is that you use that connection of yours to get the thing done. You can organise with him you take Carlos somewhere where the guy can then take over and get the thing done. You must ensure that Carlos goes with you in your car and leaves me and my car at home. It doesn't matter how it's done, but preferably a headshot with a gun. He can then be dumped somewhere along the highway. When it's done, I'll come back to Ponta and say that we had a fight and that he left me there in Nelspruit and left with a friend who I don't know. I can pay the guy after the Easter school holidays because I got a large group booking. Unfortunately, I don't have the money now. I'm willing to pay him R20 000 . . .

Number two is slightly more complicated. It doesn't need your contact and the payment, but I'd need your help. You must try and get hold of cocaine or heroin or methamphetamine or some drug and chloroform to put Carlos to sleep. You can take Carlos to your office to have the meeting there, or any other place where there aren't cameras. You need to have someone you trust . . . to help you overpower him and to knock him out with the chloroform, and then I'll inject him with an overdose of the drugs. We can then load him into the car, and I'll take him to the hospital. It will then be too late, and the cause of his death will be an overdose. Then you won't be involved in any way. I'll say that he did it himself by accident. His family will believe it because they know he sometimes uses drugs and smokes dagga.

If it can be done on Saturday, then I can drive home immediately, and I won't have to sleep over there by you. If you're not available on Saturday, you can organise it for any other day because we are available at any time, but it must please be done as soon as possible.

After all these years as a journalist, I still can't believe what criminals are willing to put down in writing. Emails, WhatsApp messages, voice notes – the incriminating details we often use to expose wrongdoing. In criminal cases, this is the kind of evidence police and prosecutors rely on to get hefty sentences.

In Maria's case, she'd left very little to the imagination, and there was no question about her intentions for Carlos. Although it was written with cold-blooded malice, in my opinion her plans were amateurish at best.

So many elements are needed to pull off a murder and get away with it. Hundreds of tiny little details could trip you up. The kinds of things you'd never even think of. But of all the glaring holes in her plan, the first and most obvious was to have put it in writing – in an email, no less.

Nevertheless, after seeing the communication, Danie knew he'd have to move quickly if he had any hopes of saving Carlos.

'She wanted to kill him and was very serious about it. And she put a lot of pressure on the informant to get someone to do it,' he told me. 'Well, my first step was registering an official case, and I got permission to do a 252A operation. And I started gathering intel on her.'

The Hawks obviously couldn't allow the murder to occur, but they would need as much evidence as possible to put Maria behind bars. Danie's idea was to use an undercover agent, posing as a hitman, to foil Maria's plans.

'We identified an agent from the DPCI to play the part, who we used to infiltrate Maria and pretend to be the hitman who would do the job for her, for the right price.'

When you look at the motives behind murders, financial gain is often at the top of the list. And in this case, the evidence points to just that: Maria was after the money. It was greed. She wanted the lodge, she wanted the money. As Gideon Jones told me, 'In the law enforcement fraternity, there is a saying that goes: follow the money. In organised crime cases, you follow the money; in corruption, you follow the money. In most crimes – follow the money. And ask yourself, who is the person who gains the most from this?'

Danie had to work quickly. His main concern was that Maria might stumble across someone who would do the job if they couldn't convince her that their undercover agent was the real deal and capable of doing the job. 'So we let the agent make contact with her telephonically. And he told her I'm your man. I'm going to do the job,' he said.

As organised as ever, Danie had offered to arrange a meeting for me with the agent during my trip to Middelburg. If the agent had been a source of mine on a story, I would have referred to him in my notes under the source name OG, Original Gangster, simply because I know he's had to infiltrate violent gangs in the past and has lived to tell the tale. When working with sensitive sources, we often give them aliases – you never know who could get hold of your notes, messages and emails. So, to tell this story, I'll call him OG.

'I played the hitman in this operation. I would have been the one who would have murdered her husband,' he told me over a cup of coffee in the DPCI's same offices.

'During the initial conversation with her, she told me quite blatantly that she wanted to kill her husband. And she would pay me R20 000, and she wanted it done as soon as possible.'

Danie says the Hawks often use undercover agents in their cases, and it's part of their mandate. But it's not something they do lightly. Infiltrating criminal syndicates, spending time with them and possibly even being part of criminal acts is a very dangerous job. And I can tell you from my own experience that it's also a job that very few people can do effectively.

Some investigative journalists use private investigators to go undercover, carry hidden cameras or audio recorders and gather evidence for their stories. I've always preferred to do it myself whenever gender, ethnicity or language barriers don't get in the way. And I can tell you that it's usually quite a nerve-wracking experience. Firstly, it's often a hurry-up-and-wait game. You rush off to meet someone and spend hours waiting for them to show, only to have them not pitch.

Criminals are highly suspicious by nature, and often it takes a few meetings to convince them that you are who you say you are. You need these people to like you, even though you might find what they do for a living detestable. You need to laugh at their jokes or pretend to be impressed with the sometimes-endless stories of brutal violence they have inflicted upon others.

At any minute, things can, and often do, go wrong. One example is from a lesson I learnt early in my career. I'd been advised to use my real name as much as possible when going undercover. And only a fake surname if I had to. But for a story in which I was looking into an alleged scammer (who thankfully wasn't particularly dangerous), a female colleague and I had gone in posing as a married couple. We'd pretended to be interested in the scammer's so-called investment opportunities and had set up a meeting.

For whatever reason, I'd given the scammer a false name and introduced myself as Michael. While he was giving us his pitch, his 2IC walked into the office and introduced himself. Getting up to shake the new arrival's hand, I naturally introduced myself by giving him my real name and asking him how he was.

As soon as the words had left my mouth, I realised my mistake. Many expletives tend to cross your mind at times like these, but I'll spare you the gory details. Luckily, my colleague was quick on her feet and expertly steered the conversation without skipping a beat. Whether the scammer realised it or not, I'll never know. He never mentioned it, and we got the footage we were after.

That's one small example of how something silly can get you into a world of trouble. I've had to try to explain to drug dealers why I didn't have the cash on me to pay for the drugs I'd just asked for, and nearly been beaten up by a giant of a man who was the enforcer for a notorious tow-trucking company when I'd posed as one of their rivals.

Police officers will tell you horror stories of having uniformed colleagues walk over to greet them while they're working undercover cases. It's a job that requires you to think on your feet and have nerves of steel.

In my experience, no matter how inconspicuous your recording device might be, it always feels as if it's sticking out like a sore thumb. And don't even get me started on arriving home to find your hidden camera had malfunctioned at a critical moment . . .

These problems could mean the difference between life and death for undercover agents like OG – their lives, and the innocent lives they are trying to protect.

'Ja, in many cases, you have to blend in with your surroundings and look like the person you're trying to portray,' OG said. In other words, you can't pitch up looking like a clean-cut kid if your backstory is that you're a street dealer. Neither can you pitch up to a meeting as a crime boss dressed like a homeless man. It's all about tiny nuances like your mannerisms and your way of speaking, and there's no formula. 'Every operation is different, and you must adapt to every one,' he said. 'Your handler, like Col Hall, will give you as much advice as possible, and together you can make many plans. But once you get there, it might be a different game.'

During his interactions with Maria, OG gave her several opportunities to back out of her plans. But she was adamant.

'She had no sympathy, no remorse. She wanted the deed done. I tried to get her to delay her trip, but she was very pushy. She set the timeline.'

Danie was surprised at just how callous Maria came across as being.

'It's interesting. I remember at one point, she asked him [OG] what's your name again? And I thought to myself, you are discussing the murder of your husband with a complete stranger over a telephone, and you can't even remember his name. But it was clear that she wanted the murder to happen, and she wanted it to happen on the specific weekend that she and Carlos were coming from Mozambique,' the colonel told me. 'So we had to organise this operation really quickly because I got the information a few days before she wanted the murder to happen. So basically, we had a weekend to put together our plan, brief our agent, and organise everything in White River, which is nearly 200 kilometres from us.'

On Sunday 19 March 2017, Danie and OG travelled to White River.

'We had organised that there would be a meeting between Maria and our agent in White River. So myself and OG drove down there and waited for her to arrive.'

The two Hawks' members had arranged to meet at a petrol station. But Maria kept trying to get OG to come to a local supermarket – not how Danie wanted things to go down.

'What happened was that Maria had driven with our informant's wife. She hadn't been part of any of the conversations, and she had no idea what was going on,' Danie said. 'They were at Pick n Pay, but we convinced Maria to attend our meeting place.'

When conducting undercover operations, police will try to minimise the risk to innocent bystanders as much as possible. A supermarket on a Sunday morning would have been much more crowded than the petrol station and presented a significantly more difficult location for the officers to try to control.

While OG stood in the parking area waiting for Maria to arrive, Danie had positioned himself in his car at a discreet angle. Both men carried video and sound recording equipment to record the meeting with Maria.

'She arrived there,' OG said, 'with another woman who was unknown to me at the time in a silver Mercedes-Benz.' In the footage Danie captured, Maria casually strolls up to OG, looking for all the world like just another tourist lazing away a Sunday afternoon in the picturesque town.

'She told me she wanted to stop along the road on their way back to Mozambique, where she wanted to buy fruit and veg from the little stalls next to the area's road.' White River is a must-see destination for many tourists, and the stalls offer locally sourced produce to eager travellers.

'I was supposed to hang around the stalls, and then as soon as I saw Maria and Carlos, I was to shoot Carlos in the head. She'd provided me with their vehicle's registration number and description. I told her, okay, I'll be sure I shoot him in the head, and suggested I shoot him twice in the head to be sure he was dead. She agreed; in fact, she was impressed with the conversation we had,' OG said.

Maria's devious plan was simple. As the couple travelled back to Mozambique, she would stop off at a specific stall where she wanted to buy some avocados. That's when OG had to strike in what she wanted to pass off as a hijacking gone wrong.

'She coincidentally, just like in the emails, told the agent to shoot him in the head again. So that tells you she wanted to be sure that her husband wouldn't survive the incident,' Danie told me. 'I thought to myself, this woman is having her husband murdered, and she's talking about avocados that she wants to buy for tonight. And then tonight she's planning on eating those avocados. And I wondered how you go and sit and eat something that you bought while your husband was lying there next to you and bleeding to death on the tar road.'

'At one stage, she asked me if I'm not from the police,' OG said. 'And I just said no, and then she just laughed about it.' Danie later gave me a screenshot, taken from OG's camera during his conversation with Maria. It's a close-up of Maria's face. She is grinning from ear to ear. It looks as though she's just won the lottery. 'She wasn't nervous or anything. She never thought twice about what she was saying. She just wanted me to ensure her husband would be shot to death.'

OG's camera also captured the moment Maria handed him R500 in cash. She'd told him she could only pay him the full R20 000 once she could claim from her husband's life insurance. The R500 was to pay for his travelling expenses because he'd told her he'd come from Johannesburg. It was another important piece of evidence for the police to gather, all pieces of the puzzle that would prove her intent.

'So I had a prearranged signal with OG to let me know that the negotiation with her had been completed . . . On that day, I was wearing civilian clothes, but I was wearing a golf shirt and cap with our Hawks' logo embroidered onto them. And as she walked away, I caught up to her and called out Maria! And she turned around quite surprised, and I told her the game was over,' Danie said. 'And she was completely shocked. It looked like her knees wanted to buckle. I informed her that this was a police operation and that I was placing her under arrest. And after informing her of her rights, we brought her into the local station where we interrogated and charged her.'

'After the arrest, I also seized her laptop. And we found more incriminating messages and emails on it, including the same email she'd sent to the informant,' Danie said.

But Maria's surprise was nothing compared to Carlos's mixture of shock and horror when he found out later that day. Danie had decided not to let him in on their undercover operation.

'I think if you have to inform someone that his wife is trying to murder him, his whole demeanour towards his wife would change. I don't think keeping your emotions in check is completely possible. You can imagine the stress that would mean for that man. So we knew we had things under control at that time and that we had a plan to protect his life, and we didn't think it would be helpful to involve Carlos before the time. We let Carlos know after the arrest and told him we wanted to see him at the police station,' Danie said. 'At White River police station, I took Carlos into my office and told him, I've just arrested your wife for orchestrating a plan to have you murdered.'

Poor Carlos was blissfully unaware of all this when he got the call. He was back at the informant's house, helping prepare for a braai the two couples were supposed to have later that day. He had no idea of what Maria had planned. He didn't even know why she'd been arrested. The informant drove him to the police station, where he eventually met a certain colonel in the Hawks for the very first time.

'I wasn't even with her,' Carlos said, back on the beach in Cape Town. 'She was with her friend. I was with the husband, waiting for them to arrive. We were going to braai and getting the fire ready and everything. And then the husband gets a phone call, and he says you know what, your wife has been arrested, and it came as a big shock to me, you know, because why would she be arrested?'

Danie remembers his first face-to-face meeting with Carlos that day in White River.

'Of course, Carlos was blown away to hear the news. And I told him this is what we had against her. And he spoke to her there in my office, but I think he was in a state of total shock. And he was more than just a little bit sceptical. But I gave him the hard facts, and told him we'd used an undercover agent and that his wife had pretty much admitted that she wanted to have him killed.'

Always quick to joke about even the direst circumstances, Carlos had a good laugh recalling the rest of his conversation with Danie.

'The colonel spoke to me and said, look, your wife wanted you killed. So you're very lucky that we came along. And I said I appreciate that, thank you very much, you know.'

More than just a little lucky. One can't help but wonder what might have happened if Maria had spoken to the wrong people and the Hawks hadn't got involved. It is doubtful that Carlos would have been around today.

'I suspect Carlos had some real marital problems, but I don't think in his wildest dreams he thought his wife was trying to have him murdered on a weekend that they came and visited people in South Africa,' Danie said.

In the run-up to her trial, Maria made several allegations that Carlos was a regular drug user and that he had mentally and physically abused her. That, she said, was the reason she wanted to have him killed. But the case against her was overwhelming, including the fact that she had planned to use her marriage certificate to get control of the lodge after her husband's death.

On top of that, investigators still had their suspicions about her previous husband's death and her possible role in it. Carlos, who continued visiting her after her incarceration, often asked about it.

'She never admitted to stabbing her previous husband, but I asked her why didn't she do a polygraph test. You know, what's funny to me is that she always refused to do a polygraph test. The test doesn't stand up in court, but it would have proved something, you know. She said no. Her lawyer advised her not to do a polygraph. And I said well, I don't understand how you can listen to the lawyer because if you want to prove that you're innocent, you'll do anything. But she never admitted, ever.'

Prof. Anni Hesselink is a criminologist at the University of Limpopo. She has gained powerful insight into the criminal mind over many years of working with the Department of Correctional Services. She's made a career out of studying some of the country's most dangerous and deranged criminals. Many of them, she's met face to face. From gang bosses to cannibals, Anni's seen it all. She's also a close friend I consulted with while writing this book.

'It is a well-thought-out plan formulated to kill her husband. It's not in the heat of the moment. This wasn't like a passion killing, where you walked in and found your husband in bed with another woman and, in a fit of rage, you shot and killed him. This was premeditated and well planned,' she told me. 'Using a hitman is a very easy way of not getting your own hands dirty. It's almost as if you won't be feeling as guilty because of your involvement in the murder because you didn't commit the act yourself. Someone else did it for you.'

In the end, Maria was charged with conspiracy to commit murder and, eventually, she entered into a plea bargain with the state. She was sentenced to twelve years behind bars.

As for Carlos, despite having narrowly escaped being murdered by his wife, life carried on. He continued visiting Maria in jail right up until she died from an unrelated illness during her imprisonment. Today, he's found new love with a woman with whom he now shares a home in the Cape.

The case is a perfect example of what proper policing should be all about. All too often, law enforcement agencies are caught on the back foot, having to respond to violent crimes after they've occurred. But with decent intelligence and the kind of men and women who are not only willing to take on crime but who are also very capable of doing so, many more murderers may just get stopped in their tracks. Colonel Hall certainly seems prepared to do just that.

'I've been a detective for 37 years and still get goosebumps when I do an operation. It is my life, it's in my blood, it's all I've known since I was eighteen years old. There are many police who don't get the recognition they deserve. Some of them have given their lives to the force. There aren't just corrupt police out there, and there aren't just bad police out there. There are police who work hard and who want to make a difference to this country. And we continue to do so without fear.'

4

THE GRANNY KILLERS

According to Prof. Anni Hesselink, the generally accepted definition of a serial killer is a person who has committed three or more murders that had either rest or cool-down periods in between. Usually (but not always), the modus operandi is similar, as is the choice of victims.

When this case first crossed his desk, Lt Col Erhard Stroh, team leader of the DPCI's Serious and Violent Crimes Unit in Mbombela (formerly Nelspruit), had no idea it would lead him on a cross-country chase, hot on the heels of a now-infamous serial killer. In fact, the morning of 9 July 2018 started just like any other for him. As was his habit, he'd gone into the office early, poured a cup of coffee and busied himself catching up on outstanding paperwork.

'At about 07:20 that morning, I was in the office at the detective branch in Nelspruit. I received a call about a murder at the Macadamia Village old age home. I took my team of detectives there, and at the scene, we found the body of the

85-year-old Hetta Potgieter.' Erhard said it was immediately clear that she had been brutally murdered: 'Her hands had been tied, there was an article of clothing forced into her mouth, and it appeared that she had been suffocated.'

I'd driven down to Mbombela to meet the wily detective on his home turf and to visit the crime scene that had kicked off his investigation. It turned out that Erhard knew Col Danie Hall quite well. They were old friends. During my visit to Mbombela, Erhard helped me find the petrol station where Danie had arrested Maria Ferreira the previous year in the nearby town of White River. If you're going to tell these types of stories, it always helps to visit as many of their locations as possible.

Like his counterpart in Middelburg, Erhard takes pride in the neatness of both his appearance and his paperwork. When I met him, he wore his silvery-grey hair in a short crew cut, with a neatly trimmed moustache and goatee. He reminded me of Richard Gere in *Pretty Woman* if you'd cut his hair to play a major in the army. The telltale lines around his dark-brown eyes hinted at a life spent witnessing some of the worst humanity has to offer. Like the scene he'd come across that morning in July.

'We immediately secured the scene and got the forensic team out. And that's where our investigation started in earnest. And that's also where I first crossed paths with the accused.'

Forensic investigator Gideon Jones will tell you that throughout a career in the police, most officers will be exposed to a lot of death. But he says it takes a special kind of police officer to solve murder cases. Having met my fair share of men and women who've done just that, I agree wholeheartedly.

Among that notable and rather small fraternity, it's often the case that murders involving the very young or the elderly provoke a particularly strong sense of duty and loyalty in the men and women investigating them. A yearning to bring some justice to a very vulnerable group of victims.

As I got to know Erhard, it became clear he'd been cut from the same cloth. Standing on the porch outside the Mbombela offices during a break, surrounded by the lush greenery of the Lowveld, I got a brief glimpse into his personal feelings about the case.

'I must say, murders committed on the elderly hit home. I always feel that someone who spent their whole life contributing to society doesn't deserve to be brutally murdered at a very high age, at a time when they should be settling down. So this was one of those cases that definitely had a big impact on me,' he said.

But what would make someone want to kill a defenceless woman in her eighties? Anni offered some insight into the possible motives of a serial killer who focused on the elderly.

'This is what makes him feel important; this gives him a sense of superiority, and this is his feeling of belonging. It's why he strangled them, forcing clothing into their mouths. It gave him so much power to see how they suffered, to see how scared they were. That fear is probably exactly what he went through as a child.' She told me to picture a Rubik's Cube with its many colourful sides. 'And as you turn the cube, you find the serial killer's typical personality traits and behaviours coming to the fore. It usually starts in their childhood years. Most of them have had traumatic childhoods, where they were either exposed to or the victims of violence and physical abuse. There's also often sexual abuse, and lastly emotional abuse.'

Erhard started his investigation with the most important puzzle piece: the crime scene.

'From a police point of view, the crime scene is where you find some of your first clues. Me and my team spent the whole day at the scene, combing through the evidence,' Erhard said. They soon discovered that Hetta had also been robbed during the brutal attack. A murder scene tells a story, and it's very important that the investigator reads that story correctly. It's the kind of skill set that sets the true greats apart from the mediocre police officers.

'While the forensic team were looking at things like fingerprints and DNA samples, we started looking at the CCTV footage from cameras inside the retirement village,' Erhard told me. This is the kind of boots-on-the-ground approach to policing that often yields the best results. Erhard immediately took control of the scene, brought in the correct units to analyse the evidence, and started following up on any leads he could.

A good detective knows he or she can't solve a case on his or her own. It involves teamwork. As Gideon will tell you, the hero cop who saves the day solo is something you'll only find in the movies.

'There's no such thing as the super detective. That concept really doesn't exist. Investigations, particularly difficult investigations, are a team effort. It's a whole group of people, each with their own unique skill sets, who are put together. And what happens then, the lead detective, the person in charge, is basically like an orchestra conductor. And those results come to him or her, and they have to put it all together.'

I drove out to the retirement village with Erhard, where we met Albert Gryvenstein, owner of a community safety project called Bossies Community Justice. The no-nonsense Lowveld local, whose gravelly voice reminded me of some of my favourite blues singers, had also raced to the scene that morning.

As the police face ever-increasing numbers of violent crimes, they need as much assistance from civil society and the private sector as possible. In the tight-knit Mbombela community, Albert often assists the police by securing crime scenes until they arrive, among other things. On the morning of the nineteenth, Erhard and his team were already on the scene when Gryvenstein arrived.

'And so I decided to see what I could do to help with the investigation. I immediately started looking at other CCTV cameras in the neighbourhood and started combing through the footage,' he said.

From my many hours going through similar footage on various investigations, I can tell you that this is another aspect of police work glamourised by Hollywood. Most CCTV systems don't allow you to zoom in to the minutest detail or have magic buttons you can push to enhance blurred images. It's simply not how they work. If the camera records in full high definition (HD) – about the best you can hope for in most South African systems – that would give you an image made up of 1 920 horizontal pixels and 1 080 vertical pixels at most. Pixels are the millions of small electronic dots that make up a digital picture. There are only so many of them in any given recorded image. They make up the details you'd want to zoom in on. And while HD video is perfectly fine for watching a movie at home, it simply doesn't record enough data for you to do much enhancing afterwards.

For example, the iPhone 15 can take a 48-megapixel photo. A single frame taken from an HD video is a touch more than two megapixels. It's the equivalent of comparing something the size of a box of matches to something the size of a box of tomatoes. You're lucky if the cameras were even switched on and recording during a crime.

Now imagine having to go through, say, twelve hours of visuals (remember, you don't know what time the crime happened, you have no description of the suspects, and you have nothing to go on) of ordinary people going about their daily lives outside a busy retirement village, and you might get an inkling of just how laborious a task this can be. But the exercise paid off for Erhard and his team.

'What we saw on the CCTV were people coming to visit their elderly relatives on a Sunday morning. There was a lot of movement. But one thing stood out. When we identified the possible suspects, they seemed completely out of place. They didn't look like people visiting their parents or grandparents. The female's clothing seemed very different from other visitors. So they caught our attention immediately, and we immediately shifted our focus on to them,' Erhard said.

In my experience, when you're trying to figure out whether a source is telling you the truth, there are often more clues to be found in what they're not saying or not doing than in what they are telling you. I've seen the footage the police went through that day in Mbombela, and the suspects didn't immediately stick out like sore thumbs. Killers don't arrive in public areas carrying large butcher's knives, wearing white ski masks and looking like Jason Voorhees in a *Friday the 13th* movie.

The suspects, a male dressed in jeans and a blue-and-white hooded jacket and a female wearing high-heeled boots, black stockings, a miniskirt and a black jacket, weren't acting particularly suspiciously. But something about them, perhaps something they weren't doing, alerted the team of investigators. One small break is often all a detective needs. In this case, the tiniest nuances in appearance and behaviour led Erhard to his next breakthrough.

'From the footage, we also identified the vehicle the suspects had arrived in. It had two different number plates on it. A Gauteng plate and a Mpumalanga plate. The one in the front, the other in the back.'

There are few things as suspicious to investigators as a vehicle fitted with contrasting number plates. The car, in this case, was a silver-grey Opel. There were now multiple red flags raised around the couple in the footage. The kinds of red flags you simply can't ignore.

'The Mpumalanga plate traced back to a caravan. So we concentrated on the Gauteng plate, which was registered to a person who lived in the Johannesburg area,' Erhard said.

On closer inspection, the team also noticed that a third male suspect had been seated in the rear of the vehicle when it left the estate. Working under Erhard's supervision, Albert shared the vehicle's details with car-tracking companies in Gauteng. He soon had feedback.

'We then learnt that the specific vehicle had a tracking device from a previous vehicle owner that had been cancelled. But we were able to get the tracker reactivated, and we could then monitor the vehicle's movements in that way,' Albert told me. It turned out that the car was on the Krugersdorp highway in Gauteng. 'Colonel Stroh and his team immediately headed towards Krugersdorp, but with their arrival in Gauteng, they were informed the vehicle had been in a bad accident a couple of hours earlier. And they found it at a panel beater's yard.'

Upon his arrival in Johannesburg, Erhard secured the vehicle and questioned the tow-truck driver who had brought in the car.

'He confirmed that he knew the driver and other people in the vehicle. So we then headed to Munsieville in Krugersdorp, where the suspects lived, according to the information.'

But who was the elusive trio the Hawks' detective had just chased for 500 kilometres to question?

'The investigation led to us finding out that the legitimate owner of the Opel had passed away and that his daughter had taken possession of it. It was the same woman we had identified on the CCTV footage at the retirement village. She was Maryna Lin Mam (47), alias Sheila Vorster. And she'd been accompanied by Shaun Oosthuizen (38) and John Leonard du Plooy (24). And our suspicion was at that time, that these were indeed the suspects we'd seen on the CCTV footage.'

The secret in cases like these is speed. The first 48 hours of a murder investigation could mean the difference between success and a cold case file. Following up on the information, Erhard and his team headed to Munsieville. I've visited this poverty-stricken suburb on the outskirts of Krugersdorp. It's not the ideal environment to spend your childhood in. Anni's Rubik's Cube comes to mind after recalling the dilapidated roads and corrugated iron shacks that are home to many of the residents.

'Then, when I turn that cube, the early childhood years cross over to a youthful person who displays behaviour that closely relates to psychopathic symptoms. Antisocial personality disorders . . . that young person usually can't accept responsibility for his behaviour. Acts impulsively. Is guilty of bullying and cruelty to others, often animals. They have no self-control. They are misleading. They lie and cheat.'

Back in Munsieville, the Hawks' team received the frustrating news that they had just missed their suspects again.

'There, we confirmed that the trio had borrowed a bakkie and that they'd left for an unknown location,' Erhard said.

But Erhard had Maryna aka Sheila's cellphone number. The Hawks have a technologically advanced cyber unit that can determine the locations of mobile phones.

'Her phone was off, unfortunately, but within the course of that week, she switched it on for a minute or two. She'd contacted her daughter. And we were then able to see in what area the phone was when the call was made. And we then headed in the direction of Rustenburg.'

It's not surprising behaviour. In fact, Erhard had counted on it. It's a phenomenon Gideon often saw in his career as well.

'A person always returns to their most ingrained habits. And one of the most basic human traits is to reach out to your family. It's human nature, and you'll find it happens in most cases.'

While Erhard's team had waited for a location on the phone, they had tracked down the owner of the bakkie, a Ford Bantam. He'd told investigators that he'd borrowed Oosthuizen's and his accomplices' camping equipment, which they'd put in the back of the bakkie.

'So we started doing basic police work and drove from camping ground to camping ground trying to find them,' Erhard said. It made sense; the team couldn't rely solely on the location from the phone. The problem with 'pinging' a phone's location, as it's sometimes referred to, is that it only gives you the location of the device at the time when it is pinged. The phone might be in a vehicle at the time of the ping, travelling along at 120 km/h. But late on the afternoon of Friday 14 July, five days after starting their investigation, the Hawks' team had a breakthrough.

'We arrived at a camping site called Lover's Rock, between Rustenburg and Magaliesberg. And we found the bakkie there. They were indeed staying in a tent. And we'd probably been watching the area for about an hour when John du Plooy left the tent to go and buy cigarettes at the café. And we grabbed him there and he became the first one who we managed to arrest,' Erhard recalled.

Du Plooy told the police officers that Shaun Oosthuizen and Maryna Lin Mam were in the tent.

'We approached the tent, not knowing if they were armed,' Erhard told me.

I've done 'ride-alongs' with the police before, joining them on some hair-raising raids. In the moments leading up to an arrest, your adrenalin is pumping. Whether you're approaching suspects inside a house, down an illegal mine shaft, or in a tent at a picturesque camping site, you never know how things are going to play out. Successful takedowns depend on the police taking control of a given situation as quickly as possible, hoping for the best but preparing for the worst.

It was a triumphant conclusion to a frustrating and sleepless week's work for Erhard and his team. 'With the help of backup police units, we overpowered and arrested them,' he informed me with a proud grin.

After an arrest, the homicide detective's job is critical. You'll separate the suspects and interrogate them individually. At that point, they're still just suspects, and you're looking to get their statements from them. You want a narrative; getting their story is important. Even if they lie, which they often do, they give you a story. The lie could be critical to your case later. You don't stop their lies; you let them talk, paint themselves into a corner, fence themselves in. If they try to change their stories later, you'll catch their lies.

'At that stage, they denied everything, of course, but we arrested them and took them to Krugersdorp [police station] where we charged them with theft and murder,' Erhard said.

It was an excellent bit of police work – the kind we need more of. Gideon agrees: 'When you're tracking someone down, you can't just stop and go home and start up again two days later. Office hours don't exist for you. That is, unfortunately, part and parcel of the job. He can't go home; he has to stay on the criminal's tracks.'

In his files, Erhard had a photograph of Shaun Oosthuizen in cuffs, staring at the camera, a police vehicle blurred in the background. The almost bald and gaunt-faced Oosthuizen has such a look of pure hatred in that image. I shudder to think what might have happened if he'd had the chance to break loose.

The speedy arrests were a prime example of how, no matter how advanced the technologies available to the police, if they're not willing to get down and dirty, they won't get far. It's also a testimony to the success achieved by cooperating with police units in different provinces, and how civil society and the private sector can contribute to the fight against crime.

Celebrating the outcome later that night, Erhard had no idea it was just the beginning of a long road he would walk with Shaun Oosthuizen. A journey into the darkest corners of a man's soul.

'When you turn that cube again,' Anni had told me, concluding her thoughts on the several aspects of a serial killer's personality, 'then another side comes to the fore. It's this really violent, aggressive person, who likes to see people suffer.

Someone who can't recognise other people's pain. Someone who has no insight or understanding of those feelings and emotions.'

All three suspects were transported to Mbombela on the weekend after their arrest, and they appeared in court on Monday morning. The case was postponed to allow the accused to apply for bail.

As the investigating officer, Erhard appeared in court over the several days for which the bail hearing lasted. He opposed bail, informing the court that due to the serious nature of the crime and the accused's subsequent behaviour, he was of the opinion that there was a valid risk of them reoffending if they were granted bail.

Our justice system is built on the principle that every person is innocent until proven guilty. During a bail application, a magistrate or judge has to make a call based on the evidence the state has at that time. Unfortunately, in this case, all three accused were granted bail.

But the case wasn't over. Erhard continued with his investigation. There is an incredible amount of paperwork that goes into a murder docket. Fingerprint reports had to be filed, DNA results requested, affidavits and statements written. It is time-consuming and laborious work, the kind of work that isn't put into the movies either. But this is perhaps the most critical part of the job.

A good defence attorney can get even the guiltiest criminal off on a technicality caused by a mistake in a police docket. I've seen it happen. It does no one any good for the police to arrest a criminal, only for them to go free after a botched court case.

But a telephone call late one weekend would blow the case wide open.

'I was relaxing at home one Sunday afternoon when I was contacted by a person who I didn't know at the time but who worked for a security company,' Erhard said. 'He'd gotten my number from someone in Gauteng. And he told me that he was standing at a crime scene in Alberton. He'd heard about our murder case in Nelspruit through the media. And he said that it looked like the same modus operandi. It was also an elderly lady; she'd also been tied up, and there was a piece of clothing in her mouth.'

The victim was 74-year-old Barbara Fenton. She'd been robbed and brutally murdered. Based on the description of the crime and knowing that Shaun Oosthuizen and his accomplices were out on bail, Erhard left to assist the Alberton detectives in Gauteng on the same day.

The man who'd called Erhard was George Moraitis, who owns and operates a large security company in Johannesburg. I met him at his offices a few weeks after my trip to Mbombela. Tough as nails and often at the forefront of the fight against crime in one of Africa's largest and most crime-ridden cities, George came across as the kind of guy you'd want to have on your side in a fight.

'The description came through that it was a white bakkie. One of the suspects had tattoos on his arms.' John du Plooy does have tattoos. Ironically, just below his neck and right next to a large design of what appears to be a koi fish, he's had the quote: 'God gives his hardest battles to his strongest soldiers' inked onto his chest.

'As a security company, we normally keep our fingers on the pulse, especially with murders like this. It was starting to look like the work of a serial killer. That's when I called Col Stroh, and I said look, I think these are the same people you're after.'

Erhard soon learnt that there were even more similarities between the cases, and a horrifying picture emerged.

'The modus operandi was that they would keep on pushing intercom buttons at the gate. Eventually, one of the residents would get so irritated that they'd open the gate. That's how they got access,' Erhard told me. It's a scary thought; they were never stopped or questioned at any retirement village. 'They would enter, and Oosthuizen would then look for units where single women lived. He'd knock on the door and ask if he could use the bathroom, and in almost all the cases, the lady would then open the door or security gate for him.'

Stacy Magid runs a marketing and PR business in Johannesburg. Barbara Fenton was her gran, and someone she loved dearly: 'She was an amazing and caring, loving person. Nothing was too much for her. She was super giving. She was kind of like our matriarch.' The news of her passing left the family devastated.

'Once they had done what they had done, and taken basically next to nothing from the house, and assaulted my gran in a horribly disgusting manner, they just left her there. We had no idea anything had occurred until the following day.'

Unfortunately for victims like Barbara Fenton, when Shaun Oosthuizen arrived at their doors, pure evil had stepped into their lives. But he could hide that fact and came across as charming and trustworthy. His victims never suspected a thing.

Whether con artists or murderers, the best criminals have a finely honed capacity to read people. They have an uncanny ability to interpret body language and manipulate situations.

Gideon says that, like predators stalking prey, they'll identify the weakest targets. 'Even a common mugger on the street will spot his victim coming past just by the way they are walking. He'll mug one person but not another, just from the body language that he's observing. In other words, the elderly are immediate targets.'

Arriving in Alberton, Erhard was informed that the same white bakkie (a Nissan 1400) the suspects had been seen in near Barbara Fenton's home had been spotted earlier the same day in a different retirement village. There, he met an elderly resident who, in all probability, is lucky to be alive today.

'I went and spoke to a lady there and got a statement from her. Shaun Oosthuizen and [John] Leonard du Plooy had come to her unit. They'd used the same modus operandi to gain access to her home, asking to use the bathroom,' Erhard told me. From their descriptions, he was sure it was the same suspects. 'I told the lady she's an absolute survivor. She'd thought incredibly fast on her feet.'

The woman in question had felt suspicious as soon as the men had come into her home and sent her granddaughter a text message.

'While they were standing right there, she sent the message. Oosthuizen did indeed, at that point, go to the bathroom. And she told her granddaughter I've made a mistake, and I've let strangers into my flat,' Erhard continued.

When Oosthuizen returned from the bathroom, she told the men it was her family on the phone and that they were at the gate and she had to let them in.

'Oosthuizen and Du Plooy then left the flat. It absolutely saved her life. The fact that she acted proactively, she realised she was in danger, and it saved her life.' Erhard paused for a second, perhaps reflecting on the miraculous escape. 'Oosthuizen literally drove two street blocks further, and they murdered Barbara Fenton later that day.'

Interestingly, Erhard later took a bottle of mouthwash Oosthuizen had used that day in the bathroom for DNA testing. The results would eventually match the DNA of the killer.

The Barbara Fenton murder occurred in September 2018, a little over a month after Hetta Potgieter had been killed in Mbombela – and while Oosthuizen and Du Plooy were still out on bail for a similar crime.

'We found Shaun Oosthuizen and John Leonard du Plooy that same week, and they were both arrested again for the murder of Barbara Fenton.'

As Erhard continued his investigation, he uncovered two more murders that Oosthuizen had committed. In June 2018, just a month before the murder in Mbombela, Oosthuizen had viciously killed 86-year-old Engela van Wyk in the same manner. And then, in August 2018, while out on bail and before the Barbara Fenton killing, 77-year-old Lillas Merry became a victim.

'So at the time, in four months, he'd committed four murders,' Erhard said.

Anni believes Oosthuizen was motivated more by the killings than the robberies, another typical serial killer trait. 'They always justify their behaviour. So, for example, they'll say I didn't hurt them that badly, I just tied them up. But if one considers that those victims were elderly people, they were fragile, they couldn't protect themselves . . . There seemed to be just absolutely no consequences to their actions. They don't care.'

Stacy Magid went to court every day during Oosthuizen and Du Plooy's trial for the murder of her grandmother. The case occurred in the Palm Ridge Magistrate's Court in Johannesburg and finished before the Mbombela case of Hetta Potgieter. Her voice verged on tears as she described the harrowing experience of seeing her gran's killer in court, apparently looking as remorseless as ever.

'To see them come in and out, see the expressions on their faces and the laughing . . . It wasn't a serious thing for them; they didn't seem to think they'd be found guilty. Completely dismissive. They genuinely didn't care.'

I've attended my fair share of court proceedings. It's another experience in which the reality is as far removed from what you'll see on television as a Boeing 747 is from a paper plane. For one, the people around you are real. Real parents who have had a child murdered. Real families reliving traumatic events. It's a heartbreaking sight. And for many of these people, it could be their first time dealing with the harsh realities of the justice system.

There are thousands of other tiny little differences you would only pick up on after spending time inside a courtroom. It's often quite difficult to hear what's being said if you're a member of the public sitting in the gallery. And much of the time in court is spent on relatively dull, albeit necessary, procedures. There are often delays. You'll rush through morning traffic to be seated as court starts at nine, only to find out that either the state or the defence is asking for a delay. All the action you'll see on those days is a judge and the opposing side's counsel checking diaries to agree on the next court date.

It's also not common for a trial to have a 'smoking gun' moment. Dramatised courtroom dramas do exactly what they're meant to do: create moments of drama. And towards the end of many shows, you'll have the 'smoking gun' moment, a scene in which all is finally revealed to the judge, jury and you, the viewer – and the bad guy is proven unquestionably guilty.

In real life, there are usually hours and hours of testimony brought by both sides. Much of it is monotonous and relatively dull. And if you're not a legal expert, you won't understand much of its implications for the trial.

So, my heart goes out to family members like Stacy. On top of everything I've just mentioned, they also come face-to-face with murderers like Oosthuizen and Du Plooy. They could be seated only a few metres apart. It's not an experience I would wish on anyone.

Erhard also attended the case; in fact, he testified in it. 'I was the last witness called, and I testified to aggravating circumstances since I already had a case against them. The trial in Nelspruit was still ongoing at the time.'

In December 2019, Shaun Oosthuizen and John Leonard du Plooy received their first convictions for the series of murders. Both men were sentenced to life imprisonment for the murder of Barbara Fenton.

During the investigations, Erhard learnt much more about how Oosthuizen operated. 'Oosthuizen stole things from the victims that he could sell. He was a regular at several fences [people who deal in stolen goods]. He would take valuables there and sell them. In one case, he got R47 000 for one of the victim's rings. After selling it, he went to a biker rally near Kroonstad. And I asked him how long the R47 000 lasted.

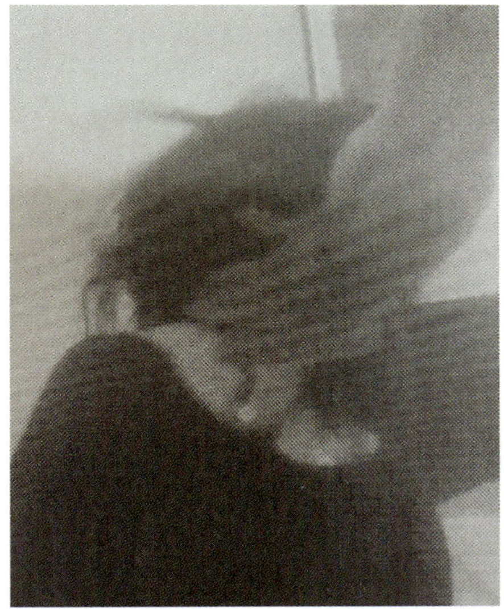

Left: The assault of the trafficked minor caught on cellphone footage.

Below: Extortion – copies of some of the messages sent to Reyneke-Bridger's victims.

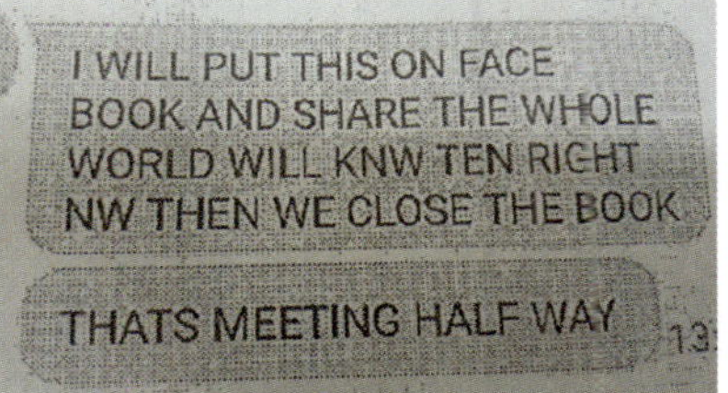

Above: CCTV cameras capture Sibanda's gang in the act.

Right: A teller is left terrorised after being held at gunpoint.

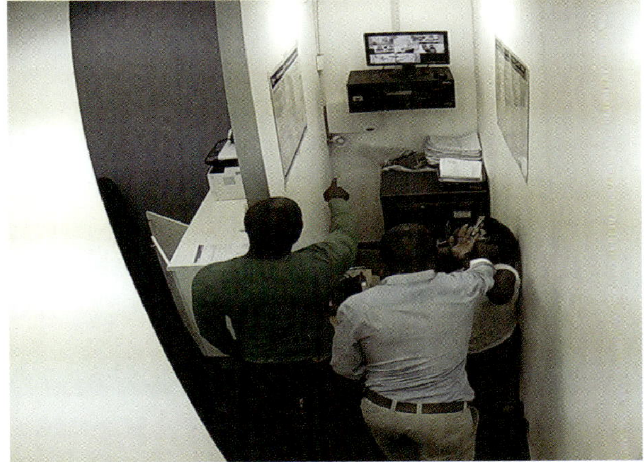

Left: Maria's big smile caught on hidden camera as she coolly discusses the hit on Carlos.

Below: Maria walking away from the undercover agent.

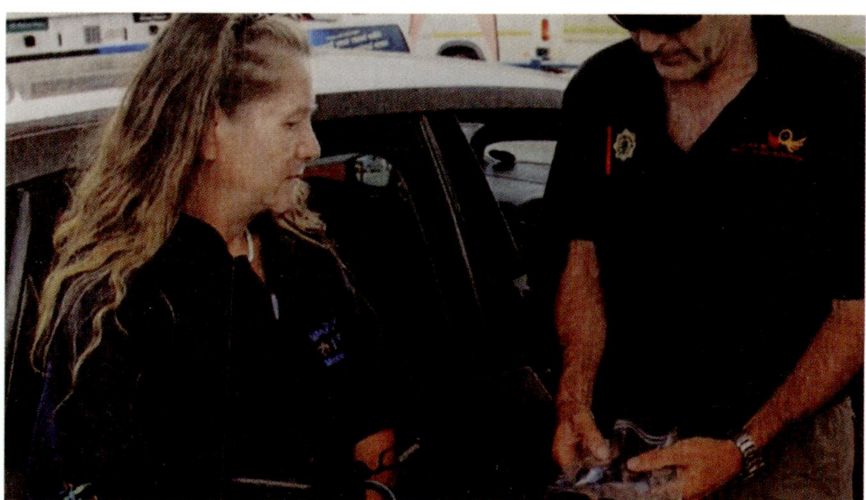

Above: The smile wiped off Maria's face after she is arrested by Col Danie Hall.

Above: CCTV footage captures the moment Shaun Oosthuizen and his companions arrive at Macadamia Village.

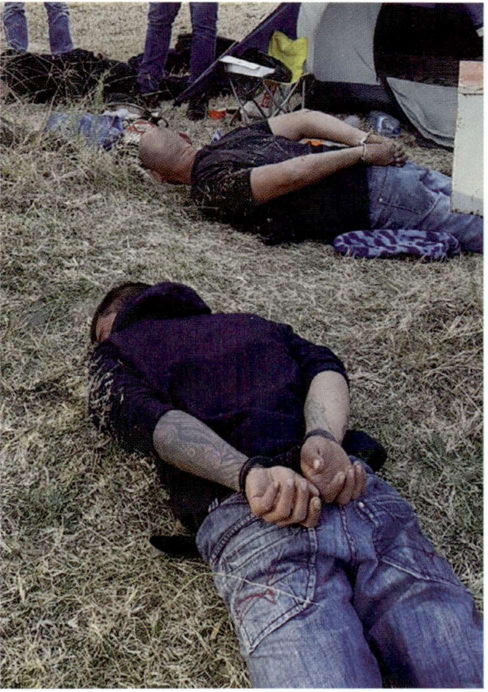

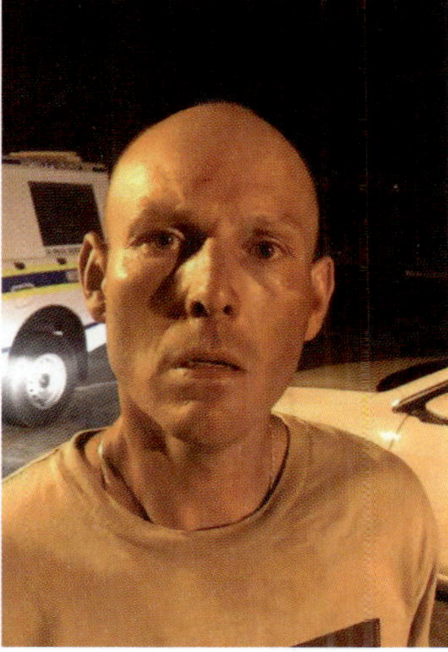

Above: The eyes of a serial killer – Shaun Oosthuizen.

Left: The trio are arrested at the camping grounds.

Above: Some of the rhino horns used in the sting operations.

Left: Huang is arrested after a joint Hawks / Special Task Force takedown.

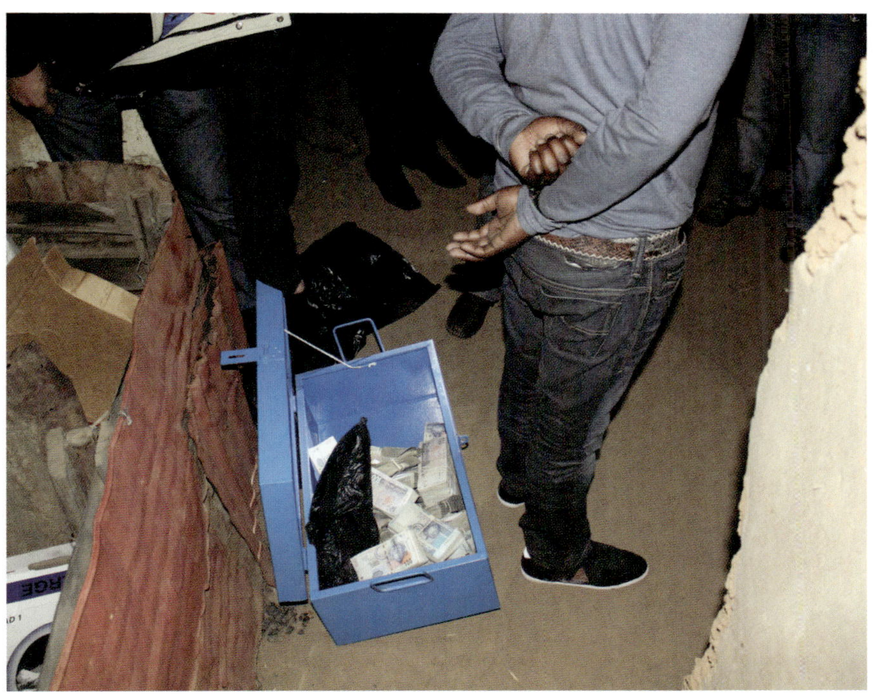

Above: One of the first suspects arrested after the R107-million cash heist.

Above: The Hawks count cash recovered from the heist.

Above: Part of Chaba's underground gold-processing facility.

Above: Rigged to explode – one of the explosive booby-traps found underground.

Right: 'Suvalos' – gold-bearing material smuggled in bottle caps.

Above: Inside an abalone-processing facility.

Above: Feng's truck seized and searched, the boxes in the foreground found filled with abalone.

Left: The hidden compartment underneath the truck.

Above: The explosive device that could have gone off during the TOMS Dalpark raid.

Left: Ending a reign of terror – some of the CIT robbers caught at the Dalpark safe house.

And he said he spent it all in a week on drugs and alcohol. Here and there, he'd bought things for his family. He blew it all in a week.'

According to testimony in several of the court cases, it was Oosthuizen who would commit the actual murders while Du Plooy ransacked their houses for valuables. According to Erhard, Du Plooy seemed to see Oosthuizen as a kind of father figure.

On 25 August 2021, Shaun Oosthuizen was also found guilty of the murder of Hetta Potgieter in Mbombela. He received another life sentence for the brutal killing.

But that wasn't the end of the road for Lt Col Stroh and the serial killer he'd put behind bars.

'One Sunday morning, my phone rang. I was hesitant to answer; it was a Sunday morning, and I was relaxing. But I answered, and a male voice on the other end of the line asked, Colonel Stroh?' The man who'd phoned Erhard was none other than Shaun Oosthuizen. 'He told me that he wanted to speak to me, that he wanted to see me. At that time, he was imprisoned in the Barberton Maximum Security Prison. And I said well, if you want to talk to me about the cases, I'll come and see you, and he said yes.'

Erhard travelled to Barberton a few days later, where he went and saw Oosthuizen in jail.

'He then told me that he wanted to get something off his chest and wanted to talk about another crime he had committed.'

I find it fascinating that, in some cases, criminals seem to latch on to the police officers who caught them. Perhaps it's because those same officers are involved in a momentous time in their lives, a time that has tremendous emotional impact.

Whether it was something about Erhard that resonated with Oosthuizen, or that he'd formed some bond with the detective, he chose the Hawks' officer as the person to whom he'd wanted to make a final confession.

'I warned him in terms of his rights, and I arranged an appointment with a magistrate in Barberton. And there he made his confession.'

Apparently, Oosthuizen had been involved in another elderly victim's death in 2015. Emma Goosen was 93 years old when Oosthuizen gained entry to her flat in a retirement home in Sunnyside, Pretoria.

'He also conned his way into her flat. He forced her into a built-in cupboard after he'd tied her up and robbed her. And then he pushed heavy furniture up against the door so that she couldn't get out,' Erhard said.

Tragically, she was only found days later. The attack happened on a Saturday, and she was only rescued the following Tuesday when staff at the retirement home found her. Erhard was obviously struggling to contain his anger as he recounted this part of the story.

'She was completely dehydrated, she hadn't eaten. But her dignity had been taken from her also. I spoke to some of her family members when I also charged Oosthuizen for this crime. And they all told me that she was a stately woman. They couldn't imagine the inhumane treatment she'd been subjected to. And yes, it was really upsetting.'

Emma Goosen succumbed to the injuries suffered during her ordeal eleven days later while she was being treated in hospital. Oosthuizen was found guilty of armed robbery in this case.

Anni wondered if his choice of victims wasn't closely related to his childhood experiences. Oosthuizen's targets were the elderly, vulnerable and defenceless. Just as he might have felt during his childhood, she speculated. But during the attacks, he suddenly had all the power and authority he'd once lacked. We may never know, but what is clear is that, just like some ravenous carnivore, he'd gone on the hunt, searching for easy prey.

'Because it's all about dominance and power for him, and here he has it now,' she said.

Shaun Oosthuizen is currently serving four life sentences for the murders of Hetta Potgieter, Barbara Fenton, Engela van Wyk and Lillas Merry. In each case, he received an additional fifteen years for armed robbery.

John Leonard du Plooy received a life sentence for the murder of Barbara Fenton, as well as an additional fifteen years for armed robbery. He got exactly the same sentence for his role in the murder of Engela van Wyk in June 2018.

The trial against Maryna Lin Mam, aka Sheila Vorster, for her role in the Hetta Potgieter murder was still ongoing at the time of writing.

During my stay in Mbombela, I'd had the opportunity to accompany Erhard in a marked Hawks' vehicle, a deceptively fast GTI. I must confess, being a huge motorhead myself, I leapt at the opportunity. Driving through downtown Mbombela with the silver-haired detective, watching the reactions of the public when they noticed that the car was a Hawks' vehicle, I'd been struck by the huge responsibility that we, as the public, place on the men and women of the DPCI. The man deftly navigating the late-afternoon traffic had certainly met those expectations in the granny killers' cases.

We had one last chat at his offices before I took my leave.

'One moment that will stay with me from the Oosthuizen case happened just after the first time we'd arrested him,' he'd said. Erhard had been transporting Oosthuizen from Krugersdorp to Mbombela to appear in court. During the journey, he'd kept asking Oosthuizen why he'd killed Hetta Potgieter instead of just robbing her.

'And I watched his eyes. He didn't answer the question, and I kept pushing him for an answer. And for a second or two, I saw the true Shaun Oosthuizen, the one the victims must have seen. I saw this aggressive character come to the fore, a character that didn't want to subject himself to authority, a man who lived a life wherein he played the most important role.'

There is such a thing as pure evil in the world, and Lt Col Stroh had come face to face with it in this case. Luckily, he's one of the few people who've made it their life's ambition to face that evil head-on. I don't know how we could sleep soundly at night if they didn't.

'I looked at him, and I saw his eyes change. His whole aura transformed to who the hell are you to ask me these questions? And I might not be in charge right now, but I'll soon show you . . . And I could really experience the despair his victims must have felt in that position.'

Looking at the photograph taken of Oosthuizen that night in front of the police vehicle all those years ago, one cannot help but agree.

5

THE HORNS OF AFRICA

What makes a good detective? It's a question I'm frequently asked. And one I've often thought about myself, to be honest. After all, some of the best investigators I know are journalists. Love us or hate us, if you want a peek behind the scenes of almost any newsworthy situation, speak to a journalist who knows their stuff. We're pretty good detectives. Although the cases we build don't have to comply with the proceedings inside a criminal court, of course.

Whole books have been written on this subject. The ability to think outside of the box often comes up. Observation skills will be mentioned. And attention to detail. They're all correct.

But the truth is, I've never met a real-life Sherlock Holmes. Detectives with fantastical abilities who can tell what time you brushed your teeth this morning from a mere glance are mostly found in the dried ink of a good book. They exist to inspire and entertain us, as well they should.

To me, the secret behind the reality of being a detective can be found in a three-step process I refer to as 'dig, connect and persevere'. DCP, if you like.

How often have you heard someone say that there were no clues left at the scene of a crime? That statement is invariably wrong. Sure, it may be true to a large degree; there were no witnesses, no DNA was found, perhaps there was no obvious motive. But what those people are either not saying or realising is that the mere fact that a crime *was* committed is the first and most obvious clue. And while we might not have any idea how, why or by whom, it offers a point of departure. A place to start *digging*.

Imagine an archaeologist in search of fossils. He wasn't around when the dinosaur he's looking for died. There were no witnesses to tell him where it happened. What he *does* know is that fossils are often found in places like riverbeds, lakes, caves and tar pits. He has a point of departure. A place to start *digging*.

That's how any good investigation starts. Like an archaeologist slowly *digging* up layers of soil, the detective needs to start peeling away the layers of a case. With each scoop of sand removed, they get closer to the truth. In a murder case, that may start with a motive. An ex-member of the now disbanded Brixton Murder and Robbery Squad once told me to find the motive. Once you have that, he said, your case is 90 per cent solved. Where you start will depend on an individual case, but do enough *digging* and you'll inevitably end up with your first decent clue.

Clues are another of those elements in criminal investigations that have been blown way out of proportion by our friends in Hollywood. The mythical smoking gun, that one clue that turns a whole investigation on its head, rarely applies in real life. But your first clue is nevertheless an important find. Hopefully, with some more *digging*, it will lead you to the next. And the next.

That's where *connecting* comes in. Since actual smoking guns are few and far between, your first clue will often set you off on a trail. Hopefully that trail will lead in the right direction. It's like the archaeologist unearthing the tip of the dinosaur's tail. He doesn't yet know where the rest of the fossil lies. But by studying his first lead, that tiny tip of information, he can make some informed decisions. Does he keep digging straight down or does he go left? Can he use a spade or is something more delicate, perhaps a brush, required?

Either way, a good detective will keep following the trail, hoping to find more pieces of the puzzle. The great detective will know how to *connect* those pieces, how they fit into each other, hopefully starting to see the picture they will eventually make up, sooner rather than later.

The final step, *perseverance*, may sound clichéd, but that doesn't make it any less true. Even more so in crime investigations. You see, all that digging, all the connecting, can often send you down a false trail. Or one that ends in a cul-de-sac. There is nothing more disheartening than spending weeks or even months on a case, only to reach a dead end. And believe me, that happens much more often than you'd think. Even worse is when what you've dug up is gold, a brilliant golden piece of the puzzle, but it's simply not enough to fill the other blanks.

So, what does the archaeologist do when he's spent months excavating the tip of that tail only to find that the rest of the fossil is missing? He starts digging again. Somewhere else, this time. Perhaps a little further down the ancient riverbed. Maybe the flood that killed his T-rex millions of years ago displaced some of the skeleton. Maybe not. There's only one way to find out. *Perseverance.*

Why am I telling you all of this? The next case we're going to look at has many of these elements. It involves a detective doing some digging. A detective you've already got to know, in fact. And it's about how one clue from one crime led him down a trail to another, much bigger, find. It also involves the skeletons of animals. To be more precise, the horns of those animals. While this species didn't become extinct millions of years ago, it's come close to the brink.

'When the tragedy hit South Africa – when we first realised just how big a problem rhino poaching had become – it was a very difficult situation.' Col Johan Jooste is the National Commander for the Hawks' Wildlife Trafficking Unit. He was the man tasked with the unenviable job of combatting the scourge of rhino poaching that hit South Africa from about 2008. 'There were a lot of emotions. We were told to stop this at all costs. We had to stabilise the situation.'

I first met the colonel at Wachthuis, the head office of the SAPS. It was a typically hot day in downtown Pretoria. Walking down the main corridor leading to the unit's offices, I was pleasantly surprised. It looked like you would expect a wildlife trafficking unit to look. Walls, doors and whiteboards were covered in posters and photos, most of them depicting endangered fauna and flora. Others offered grim reminders of humanity's greed – the willingness to exploit our wildlife at any cost. Rhino horns. Pangolin scales. Lion bones.

As with most of the priority crimes the Hawks' investigate, the illicit wildlife trade is dominated by organised crime

syndicates. They've long ago realised just how valuable a commodity some of South Africa's indigenous species are. They'll stop at nothing to get it.

Johan looks like he could be a rugby player, and wouldn't have looked out of place running onto the field with Siya and his squad at the 2023 Rugby World Cup. With his broad shoulders and thick neck, he'd make a formidable opponent in any contact sport. From my own experience, I'm well aware of just how dangerous the world of rhino poaching has become. The syndicates behind the crimes won't hesitate to eliminate anyone they deem a threat. So, over a mug of coffee kindly supplied by Johan's assistant Alta (who, I later learnt, doubles as the unit's mother hen and general problem solver), that's where I started the conversation. I wanted to know how dangerous things really were.

'Unfortunately, when there is money, power and greed, people are even willing to take on law enforcement with violence,' he told me. 'And that's the reality we have to deal with.'

It's a reality Col Danie Hall knows all too well. I was pleasantly surprised to find out that for this story I'd be dealing again with the veteran investigator I'd met a few months ago while researching the Carlos Ferreira case. Danie had worked on several cases with Johan while he was still at the Organised Crime Unit. And a few years ago, he lost a close friend who'd been looking into a rhino-poaching syndicate.

'My friend and colleague Lt Col Leroy Bruwer,' Danie recalled, 'was the investigating officer on a rhino case we had codenamed Project Broadball. The focus was on a dangerous rhino-poaching syndicate. The investigation was taking place at a very high level,' he told me. But in March 2020, at the height of the investigation, the unthinkable happened.

'He was shot and killed on his way into the office, in what was an obvious hit,' Danie said. It was clear that the tragic incident still haunted Danie. One picture from the crime scene showed the white sedan Leroy had been travelling in that day. At least four bullet holes riddled the windows on the right side, obviously made by a high-calibre weapon: a stark reminder of just how ruthless the criminals behind poaching syndicates can be.

'Their intelligence structures rival our own in terms of capabilities,' said Johan. 'And they're constantly attempting to counter any initiatives we launch.' Danie agreed. He'd travelled from his offices in Mpumalanga to Pretoria the previous day to attend to another case. But that morning he'd shown up at headquarters dressed to a tee again, in a cream-coloured jacket complemented by a brightly striped red-and-black tie. Again, I couldn't help myself from being reminded of a certain Mr Bond from Her Majesty's Secret Service.

He'd agreed to join us and take me through a case the Hawks had codenamed Project Python. Danie had been the investigating officer on the case, while Johan was the commanding officer. It all started in January 2018, when the team received info from a confidential informant.

'The information was that a Chinese national, a certain Mr Feng, was going to buy a rhino horn illegally. He didn't have the required permits to make the purchase,' said Danie. It was still two years away from the fatal attack that would cost his friend Leroy his life.

'And we set a trap for him. Myself and Lt Col Bruwer. We waited for him in the early morning hours in Middelburg. He arrived in a white vehicle, and we stopped him.'

Feng was detained, and his car was taken to the Hawks' offices in Middelburg.

'We contacted our Forensic Laboratory in Pretoria, and Colonel Espag and his team came out to inspect the car. And they found a rhino horn hidden beneath the vehicle, in between the chassis,' Danie recalled. Feng was arrested and charged for the crime.

Danie took me through some photos of the arrest. One of them gives you a hilarious insight into the criminal genius of Mr Feng. The rhino horn they found hidden in the car was in a large hessian bag. Written across the outside in large capitals that could only have been made by a permanent marker was the word 'COW'. How anyone could have thought this would be enough to throw law enforcement off their tracks is beyond me. Truth, as the saying goes, really is stranger than fiction sometimes.

But what the Hawks now had was a place to start *digging*. Johan and Danie's idea was to use Feng to lead them up the chain of command of the syndicate. After he was released, they put him under surveillance. Their efforts paid off; Feng led them straight to his bosses in the syndicate.

'The plan was to eventually also charge Feng under Project Python,' Danie laughed. 'But before that could happen other members of the Hawks caught him again. In another operation. He was in possession of rhino horn and seahorses. So he was arrested and he eventually did jail time for those crimes.'

The surveillance on Feng had led the team to Johannesburg, where he was delivering rhino horns to his superiors. Danie got together with an ex-Hawks' colleague Johan Brits, who was at that stage employed by South African National Parks (SANParks). They'd also been looking into Feng's activities.

'And we sat around a table and decided to investigate the rest of the syndicate, their hierarchy. And that's how Project Python started. It would be run from Mpumalanga and focus on the role players in Johannesburg, who had the market there,' Danie said.

Like most of the units in the DPCI, the team's idea was to focus on the bigger fish.

'The role of Wildlife Trafficking within the DPCI is to look at syndicates,' Johan explained. 'We look at how the syndicates place themselves in the provinces, how that links in at a national level, and then eventually how it ends up at the end user internationally.'

With rhino horn, it's almost always a case of cross-border smuggling. 'The market is in Asia,' Danie said. 'We don't really have a market for illegal horns in South Africa, we don't have the end users. But there is an international demand, and as long as there is a demand, that demand will be satisfied.'

The Hawks classify the players in the illegal trade according to levels. Level one, two and three are considered the bottom of the rung. These are typically the actual poachers, the men who will go into the bush and hunt the rhinos. They are merciless, and the poor animals are often subjected to unnecessary violence. A few years ago, at the height of the rhino-poaching epidemic, some game rangers in our national parks were getting PTSD from having to attend to multiple poaching scenes every other day. To add to the trauma, they were facing well-armed poachers who wouldn't hesitate to shoot to kill. Remember, these were game rangers, trained in wildlife conservation. Not bush warfare. While researching a possible story on the subject, I once spoke to a game ranger who'd had a terrifyingly close call. He'd been on the spoor of a rhino they'd suspected had been wounded during an attempted poaching incident. While trekking through the thick undergrowth, he'd heard an ominous noise. The unmistakable metallic click of a gun being cocked. A well-camouflaged poacher was hidden in the bushes somewhere close by. Alone and possibly outgunned, the ranger had thought on his feet and simply continued on his way as if nothing had happened. All the while expecting a bullet to the back. Luckily that didn't happen, and the poachers were later tracked down by law enforcement.

Violent as they may be, the lower levels aren't the ones earning the big money. They might get paid about R35 000 a kilogram for rhino horn. That price keeps going up the higher in the syndicate you move. If they can successfully smuggle the horn overseas, the syndicates can easily make R140 000 a kilo. And that's where you'll find the kingpins.

'They're making millions worldwide with the smuggling of rhino horns,' Danie said.

And that was the idea behind Project Python: to keep digging until they could find the level fives, sixes and sevens. The plan was to infiltrate the Johannesburg syndicate members with an undercover operation.

'We put together a multidisciplinary team,' Danie said. 'We set goals to achieve, we had a whole group of role players on board to help. We had a dedicated state prosecutor on board from day one. And then of course you choose your investigating methods. And we decided to send in an undercover agent.'

It would be a difficult and dangerous task. The smugglers are highly professional and organised. They're also well funded and usually armed, said Johan.

'They get paid for it, and they get paid a lot for it. That's what makes it difficult and that's where the danger comes in. These guys, and the structures they set up, they don't want us poking our noses in there,' he said. 'They actually go out and launch counterintelligence operations against law enforcement efforts. Whether it's normal patrols or roadblocks. Or provincial or national projects. They're too used to the money. They'll pay anyone, to do anything.'

Danie told me the surveillance on Feng had provided a single critical clue about the Johannesburg syndicate members.

'We were able to identify one of the role players. At that time, we only had an alias. He was known to us as the Old Man.' The Old Man was the person to whom Feng was supposed to deliver the rhino horn. 'We obtained 252A authorisation from the office of the Director of Public Prosecutions. And the NPA also provided us with an excellent state prosecutor, Advocate Marlie van Heerden in Johannesburg. She would oversee all the legal landmines.'

The plan for the undercover operation was to let the Hawks' agent make contact with the Old Man, posing as a seller.

'So our agent made contact with the Old Man. He was later identified as Eugene Huang. A Taiwanese citizen,' Danie said. 'And our agent was able to meet him. And from the conversations they initially had, it was clear that he was our guy. He was in the market for illegal rhino horn.'

The agent wore a hidden camera during the operations, and Johan and the team gave me access to some of the material. Wearing the camera, of course, made the operation all the more dangerous. In the footage, Eugene Huang looks like any other average man you'd see on the streets of Joburg. The nondescript Taiwanese man has black hair, and is of average size and build. The only immediate conclusion to be drawn from first seeing him is that he probably has bad eyesight. In nearly all of the clips, Huang is wearing a pair of prescription glasses. But he was hungry for business, and during one of the conversations he told the agent that he was supplying some big-time players. 'These buyers,' Huang explained in somewhat broken English, 'they're going to get 100 or 200 kilograms per month, no problem, okay?'

I had also discussed this case with Gideon Jones, of course – as the former head of the police's undercover operations, this type of work was his bread and butter.

'When the goal of your operation is to gather evidence against the higher-level syndicate members,' he told me on one particularly chilly winter's day in Pretoria, 'one of the most effective, and often the only, ways of doing that, is to let an undercover agent infiltrate the gang.' Despite the bitterly cold wind howling outside, Gideon was dressed in his customary khaki short-sleeved shirt and a pair of blue jeans. I'm willing to take a bet that if you ever run into him on the street, he'll be similarly attired. And he'll have his trusty 9mm Sig Sauer pistol concealed at his side. Personally, I'm a fan of the Czech armament manufacturer CZ. But Gideon says the Sig is the Rolls-Royce of pistols. Anyway, that's his look. I've teased him about it. He likes it. He's told me so.

'It's not everyone's cup of tea to be an undercover agent,' Danie had told me back at Wachthuis. That, as Lee Child's famous character Jack Reacher would say in one of his novels, is for damn sure. 'Agents are chosen for the work they do,' he said. It's a deadly game of cat and mouse. Get it wrong, and the consequences could be permanent.

'You need to be very careful when you're using a police-man as an undercover agent,' Gideon had said. 'The reason is actually very simple. They are only human. And humans aren't equipped to be absolutely resistant to everything that comes their way. In other words, an agent can all too quickly get drawn in, becoming the character they're playing.'

That's why the police seldom send agents in undercover for extended periods. Except for the obvious difficulties it creates operationally, they are exposed to a lot of temptation. The high life. Fast cars, tons of cash. It's all there for the taking.

Anni says those aren't the only temptations. For an agent to successfully infiltrate a criminal organisation, they need a backstory – a term writers often use for the history and background they create for their fictional characters. The police create these backstories to make their agents seem believable to the syndicates they need to infiltrate.

'A pseudo-identity is created,' Anni told me. 'The goal is for them to appear appealing to the criminals. To be accepted. To be trusted.' That's what the police want, of course. But Anni says it's not uncommon for agents to develop strong bonds with the people they are investigating.

'When an agent has been accepted into the fold, you'll find that they become a part of the gang's social structure. And interestingly, the social side of crime is an even bigger part of that lifestyle than the criminal side.' Anni says that could be anything from joining family gatherings to drinking together. The agent has to stay in character. And while doing so he or she will get to know the syndicate members intimately.

'They've worked themselves in, they have a legend behind them,' Anni said. 'It's like something out of one of the *Godfather* films. And the agent becomes part of those structures. And you would think they're family.' What law enforcement needs to be wary of in these situations is the agent becoming too emotionally invested in his or her target. Real friendships develop. Love might blossom. Trust me, it's all happened before.

'Our agent's legend was that he was a corrupt official,' Danie explained. This made a lot of sense. In real life, the man worked for SANParks. So, if Huang or anyone else in the syndicate were to do some digging, that's what they would find. You don't want your agent's backstory to be checked out and found to be fake. 'The agent supposedly had access to stockpiled rhino horns in SANParks. The syndicate loved it. He told them he could get a lot of it.'

Danie said their agent had initially taken things slowly. He'd befriended Huang. There were lots of WhatsApp messages sent. Some friendly meetings where they discussed the possibilities. From the hidden camera footage, it was clear that Huang was getting more and more excited about his corrupt official and the potential source of horns.

'So no risk,' he said on one occasion. 'We check here, then we bring the money here, then go.' The agent had clearly won Huang's trust. Huang was in fact trying to set the agent's mind at ease. 'So we come here, we check it. Money paid. Money is waiting now. So it's much easier. Everyone, no, no risk.' Huang was even taking the agent out to lunch; in some of the footage, Huang introduced him to a soup he enjoyed in a Chinese restaurant.

'Eventually the agent set up a sale. And in May 2018, he sold two horns to Eugene Huang.' The transaction was also caught on camera. In the footage Huang and another man, hitherto unknown to the agent, can be seen inspecting the horns closely, verifying their authenticity. Huang wanted it to appear that he was a middleman for a buyer, and negotiated with the agent for his commission. 'Okay then the rest,' Huang said, 'you get that. All right? So you get R480k for us, for the big one. I get . . . but then for you it's R450k instead.' Because Huang kept referring to a buyer, the Hawks had to try to get him to reveal the person's identity. But it was still early days. So, they let the transaction go ahead.

'So Eugene's modus operandi was that he would meet the agent at a certain place in Johannesburg. Then he would take him to what we call a safe house. It had high walls, electric fencing, CCTV cameras,' Johan recalled. This first encounter was one of the most stressful parts of the operation. The rest of the Hawks' team could only wait nearby; the agent had to go in alone. No one knew what to expect. It's something Gideon has dealt with often enough.

'It's a very difficult situation. Very few people can really do it. And it's extremely dangerous. So you can't send in some-one who doesn't have the skills to read the situation correctly, to handle it correctly and to do the correct things.' Even Huang seemed nervous. And ironically, even though he was a criminal himself, he was worried about being robbed.

'For Chinese people it's not safe. It's really not safe,' he told the agent. 'They will rob you. These town people they rob you. If you have cash, they get some cash. And try to search and pinch some cash.'

Danie remembers the first sale clearly. 'He went into the premises, and inside the horns were handed over. They dis-cussed the price. Once they agreed, the agent had to wait for the cash to be brought to the house. After the cash was handed over, our agent climbed into his car and left. And Eugene Huang stayed behind with the horns.' Danie, who had also been the agent's handler during the operation, admits there was a big sigh of relief among the team when the agent arrived back safely.

'Ja, it's nerve-wracking. As the investigating officer I'm not directly involved during the transaction. So I'm waiting nearby, and I'm worried. Is the agent okay, did the transaction happen, did everything go to plan?' The truth is that during the transaction, there isn't much protection for the agent. They only have their wits to rely on. 'For those few hours you can only sit and wait. And be patient.'

In the footage, it was clear that Huang and the unidentified man knew their stuff. The horns were inspected closely. Samples were sawn off and tested. They also haggled about the price, Danie said.

'They inspect the product. And then they negotiate. They'll say but this horn isn't good quality, there's a crack in it here. These pieces are dead pieces. Then they'll remove those pieces, they just used a hammer. And then they inspect it again.' Huang was most likely also checking the horn for any hidden tracking devices perhaps planted in the horns by the authorities. They'd also want to make sure that the horn hadn't been treated with any chemicals that would make it unusable. Some South African game farmers have reportedly tried adding poisons to the horns to prevent poaching. During the inspection, Huang told the agent: 'We have to worry about your side. You don't get a trick. You don't get anything funny. Right?' Once the men were satisfied, they'd offer the agent an amount per kilogram.

'So part of our article 252A authorisation was to use real rhino horns that were stockpiled for the transactions,' Danie said. 'We simply can't try and sell them false horns. These guys are professionals. They know exactly what to look for. So you have to supply them with a real horn.'

During the first operation, Huang paid the agent R470 000 for the two horns.

'Of course, the money is evidence in our case. So the agent is in control of that money until I take it into custody. Then we count the money, note the serial numbers etc. And the cash is paid into a bank account for safe storage, and it becomes part of the evidence that the state will present in its case,' Danie explained.

Johan says that operations like Python are having more and more impact on the illegal industry. 'We're hitting them where it hurts. When these operations are successful they lose a lot of cash. And we're becoming more and more successful. Our turnaround time with the syndicates and these complicated kinds of investigations are getting so much better.'

After the first sale went down in May, the investigation focused on identifying the second man. And they soon had a name.

'He was Shiuhau Chen,' Danie said. 'He was a Chinese national. He was the guy who inspected the horns. And he was present during all the sales at the safe house. He was also the guy who would leave with the horns and come back with the cash.'

With his heavyset build and crew-cut hairstyle, Chen could easily play the stereotypical thug in a martial arts movie. He looks dangerous. In the hidden camera footage, he almost never speaks. He's all business. Huang, on the other hand, played the part of the friendly broker. After the success of the first transaction, the agent had Huang in the palm of his hand. And the Hawks found out just how big a player he really was.

'Now how many kilograms can you get?' He asked the agent at one point, pen and notepad in hand, 'How many kg [pronounced "kay gee" by Huang] you can carry at a time? For example, I don't know whether you agree or not. If you don't agree, no problem, is that if you bring 100 kg, they'll pay you 35 kg, 35 kg. In a few days. If you carry 100 kg, 100 kg is probably worth how much? R5 million. R6 million.' The syndicate was greedy. And it had huge amounts of cash. Huang never displayed any emotions towards the poor animals he was exploiting. He might as well have been discussing bags of soil.

In the past decade, more than 9 000 African rhinos have been killed for their horns. That number is probably a lot higher by now. That's nearly one rhino every day. All of it driven by an insatiable market in the East.

The Hawks could have arrested Huang and Chen during the first sale. But they decided not to. They were still *digging*. And *connecting*. Danie said it was all part of a bigger strategy.

'Our strategy is always to look at how many of the syndicate members we can identify. To look at the money flows. The money laundering. So for us it was necessary to do more than one transaction. We wanted to see how high up the chain we could go.' Having more than one purchase would also later help prove the case in court. The syndicates can afford the best lawyers money can buy. The Hawks wanted to avoid the defence trying to play the 'this was a once-off deal' card. They team wanted to prove a criminal enterprise. 'We don't just do these cases willy-nilly. We had the state prosecutor on board, and we had our strategy. In this case we ended up doing three transactions.'

The second sale took place at the same safe house a few months later. Chen's role was becoming more and more evident. He was there again to inspect the horns. Once happy, he took them and disappeared. In the footage, Huang and the agent can be seen going to a restaurant for lunch while they wait. When Chen came back, all three men again met at the safe house. This time around, they paid the agent R1,2 million in cash for the four horns he'd brought. Danie says by now Chen and Huang were quite trusting, but no less paranoid.

'Like I said, these guys were professionals. So they told the agent to be careful of who he spoke to. Not to trust anyone. They told him what type of cellphone he should use. They even gave him a SIM card for the phone. They told him to use the SIM card to stay under the radar.' Huang insisted that the agent use an older-model cellphone. Apparently, he believed the older phones couldn't be traced by law enforcement. The agent was only to use the older phone and the provided SIM card to contact him. The SIM card wasn't registered under anyone's name with local cell providers, and was therefore untraceable to any one individual. Meanwhile, the agent's camera was capturing it all.

'Okay, and also the cellphone,' Huang said. 'I'll give you the SIM card. The SIM card no register. So when you go back, you spend few hundred and you get Nokia. Not smartphone. Nokia. Whenever you left your area, you use the Nokia to talk, okay? So then it's easier, for him also Nokia [pointing at Chen]. So it's the three of us, no one can trace.'

Although he tried his best, the agent never managed to get Huang to open up about the mysterious money men, the people supposedly paying Huang for the horns. It is possible that this was all subterfuge on Huang's part. He and Chen may have been at the head of operations on the South African side. But the sting operations did help uncover the money-laundering side of the syndicate's operations. And once again, it all happened on camera.

'And then after that we go casino,' Huang is heard saying in the footage, just as the agent was about to leave. 'And then when you're ready, we come back.' This was an unexpected turn of events. Huang wanted to take the agent to a casino, to show him how they laundered the money. It was one of those out-of-the-blue occurrences that every undercover agent will face at some point. Going off script can significantly increase the danger. But it can also yield rich rewards in terms of new evidence. The agent made the call and agreed to accompany Huang to a casino in Johannesburg.

Money laundering is big part of organised crime. Syndicates do their best to make it seem like the funds they have access to have come from legitimate sources.

'So you go to the casino and you open an account there,' Danie explained. 'Those accounts are there for gamblers who want to deposit funds with the casino to use whenever they come in. On that day they opened the account in the agent's name, and they helped him in the process, and facilitated it. And the money that had been paid for the rhino horn on that occasion was paid into the account.' Criminals will declare the funds as income from gambling if the authorities ever check. This is an old and quite common form of money laundering that I've come across several times. The casinos don't know where the money comes from. The criminals will deposit, withdraw, gamble some of it. All in an attempt to hide its origins.

An illicit gold dealer, who sometimes used the same method, once told me it was like having a 24/7 bank account. The casinos are always open, and you could walk in and access large amounts of cash at any time without raising eyebrows. 'And who knows,' he said slyly, 'you might even win a few million on top of it all.'

At the casino, the agent met a third player in the syndicate. A female, whom the Hawks would later find out was also a Chinese national and Huang's life partner.

'Her name was Ping Wu,' Danie told me. 'She was Eugene Huang's girlfriend. And she was a role player in the money laundering. She opened the account for the agent. They also gave our agent two casino cards. One was worth R50 000, the other R25 000. And that also became evidence in the case.'

Meanwhile, Eugene was increasing the pressure on the agent – he wanted bigger deliveries. At one point he said he could buy 200 kg at a time.

'They only payment in a month's time. 200 kg all finished. Can you do that?'

'The constant pressure on the agent was taking its toll. Huang was putting a lot of pressure on him,' Danie recalled. 'The whole time, he just wanted horns. Once he'd seen that we could deliver, that's all he wanted.'

'Can you make it once a week coming here?' Huang asked in another clip. 'Once a week coming here, one time, just finish, then go? It become a routine. You just tell me how much, just like this [pointing at the horns] I will . . . we can get that from . . . from . . . I will convince the buyer, just prepare the money. You come, wait, then money's here, go.'

'Of course we didn't deliver horns to him each time he asked. But during the third and last transaction in September 2018 we sold him six horns,' Danie said. 'That was also worth more than a million rand, that he put down on the table in an ordinary rucksack.'

Having got no further up the chain, the Hawks had decided it was time for the takedown.

'You have to plan these arrests very carefully,' Danie said. 'The plan was to arrest them in the act. So although he had the horns with him the transaction was never completed. So on the day we had our teams in place, including members of the SAPS Special Task Force.'

The Task Force was there to add an extra level of safety during the arrests. They're a specially trained elite unit, and they handle the most dangerous and difficult police operations – like hostage situations. I've seen them in action. They don't take nonsense.

'The reason they were there,' Gideon told me later, 'is exactly because there is so much violence associated with the illicit rhino trade. They're going into the safe house, and they don't know what they're letting themselves in for.'

Danie said they'd spent a lot of time going over the plan, getting operationally ready.

'We briefed them on the address, the location. We looked at the risks associated with the area. The agent filled us in on what the place looked like inside. So there's a lot of things the Task Force look at before we go in. Their job is to ensure the safety of my team, and of course to prevent the suspects from getting away. And I must admit, you do feel pretty safe when you have these guys on your side. You're minimising the risks to your team. And afterwards, we know we can safely do our work at the crime scene.'

Luckily, both Huang and Chen were arrested without any incident.

'My colleague, late Col Leroy Bruwer, went to Eugene's house at the same time. And he arrested Huang's life partner

Ping Wu,' Danie said. She was eventually charged for her part in the money-laundering operation.

After the arrests, the Hawks searched Chen's home.

'And in the home,' Danie said, 'we found a .22 calibre pistol in a small case. And it had a silencer attached. Because other people had access to the weapon in his home, he was never found guilty on that charge. The magistrate gave him the benefit of the doubt. But the question remains, what would anyone be doing with a .22 pistol, with its serial number filed off, and with a silencer on it, in the middle of downtown Johannesburg?'

Danie was successful in opposing bail for all three accused, and they were kept in custody until their trials. Huang never made it to trial. A short while before his case was heard, he passed away from natural causes. Chen tried appealing the bail ruling in the High Court, but his application was denied.

'Ping Wu's testimony was that she hadn't understood what was happening between Eugene and our agent,' Danie said. 'She said she'd been present during one or two dinners they'd had. But she said she couldn't understand their conversations, because she couldn't speak English.' But Danie and the Hawks' team had access to her cellphone, and they found many of the messages on the phone were in English.

'And we realised that she had opened a police case in 2008, she said she'd been assaulted. And her affidavit was made in English, without a translator being present,' Danie said.

This cast serious doubt on her version, and Danie had his team track down the constable who had taken her statement at the time.

'We let the constable who was on duty all those years ago come and testify in the case. And it was obvious that Ping

Wu was lying. She was in fact quite capable of following the proceedings in English. And at the end of the day the magistrate completely rejected her version.'

Johan had a rather singular take on Wu's case.

'I called Ping Wu the five-step suitcase carrier. She was involved on the money-laundering side. She wasn't all that involved in the other dealings. But because we explained her role to the court, she received a five-year sentence for money laundering.'

Chen was found guilty on three charges for the illegal buying and possession of rhino horn. He received a five-year sentence or R500 000 fine. He was also given two years' imprisonment without the option of a fine. The magistrate also ordered that he be deported back to China once his sentences had been served. Unfortunately, both Huang and Chen had played their cards close to their chests – the Hawks never did find any other syndicate members directly connected to their operations. The case, to me, is a classic example, though. They did some *digging*. They did some *connecting*. Good, old-fashioned police work that led to solid results. For Johan and the Wildlife Trafficking Unit, it's just another day at the office. Their job is to *persevere*.

'In this case the casinos gave us their cooperation. The banks. We all worked together to put this in front of a judge. And the case against Ping Wu will send a clear message. The magistrate understood what they were doing. It was money laundering. Five years for five steps. That's a good sentence,' he said.

Both he and Danie had just finished a much bigger operation, called Project Blood Orange, when I'd been to see them. A whole lot of the work done there still needs to be ventilated in the courts, so unfortunately I couldn't add it to this book. But they did give me some insights into the case.

'We've just finished with Blood Orange,' Danie said. 'Like with all organised crime, there is a lot of corruption that's involved in the rhino horn trade. Our information led us to corrupt game rangers. They were accepting money from the syndicates, for information on where to, for example, find rhino in our national parks. Information about patrols, when they took place, where. So we've arrested sixteen suspects. Many of them rangers. And some of their family members who were also involved.'

Johan said Blood Orange looked at the corruption, the money laundering and how it was influenced by the poaching activities inside the Kruger National Park. When he explained it to me, he started off with a statement I've heard all too often on organised crime cases.

'It is unfortunately the case that organised crime cannot happen without some form of corruption. So when we started identifying people, unfortunately we came across quite a few who were employed by the Kruger National Park.' The Kruger is the largest game reserve in Africa – nearly two million hectares of untouched biodiversity. It was one of the hardest-hit places when the rhino-poaching pandemic reached South Africa. Some reports estimate that the White Rhino population in the Kruger has decreased by 75 per cent since 2011. Today, there are only about 2 600 White Rhino left in the park. Even fewer Black Rhino, at about 200.

'We found rangers,' Johan said. 'Veterans in the park, who'd been bought. They'd accepted bribes. They were selling info. For instance, about the patrols, when they were taking place, and where. So when you have people like that working against you, it's part of the collapse of this whole philosophy of protect the rhino.'

Anni says morals fall by the wayside when money is at stake. Especially easy money. The worst part is that once you've accepted a bribe, the syndicates have you where they want you.

'When you're in, you're in. They know too much about you. They have dirt on you. It's like being part of a gang. In the beginning the lifestyle seems very alluring. Everybody wants to be your friend. But the reality is simple. You are just being used.'

I've seen this so many times in my career. It's easy to take the moral high ground: I wouldn't accept the bribe, I'd protect the animals. The reality is that protecting the animals doesn't always pay enough to cover the school fees. Medical bills. Feed the hungry mouths. Many of the game rangers come from the extremely impoverished communities you'll find on the outskirts of the Kruger Park. And it's here that I feel one of the most overlooked aspects of the rhino-poaching problem can be found.

I've been to some of these communities. People live in shacks. They don't have access to running water. They don't have electricity. Jobs are scarce. Children walk kilometres to go to schools that still use pit toilets. Imagine living like that. The closest you'll ever get to the Kruger is seeing the rich and wealthy driving up to the entrance gates. It's an exclusive world to which you're barred access. The ticket price for a day visit exceeds what you'll earn in a week. Or a month. So just how hard would it be to convince you to take part in poaching? The horn from one rhinoceros will pay you a year's wages. For the game rangers who come from these communities, life is not that much better. Sure, they earn a salary. But they have families. Parents and siblings – whole communities living on the breadline. And then I ask myself, where have all the hundreds of millions, much of it from the international community, raised in the fight to save our rhinos gone?

I don't have the answers. I'm also not condoning the mass killing of our wildlife for monetary gain by ruthless criminals. But until the country can find answers to these complex socio-economic issues, all the law enforcement efforts in the world won't save our rhinos.

Johan says moral corruption is not the only problem. They've had cases where people had been coerced into doing the bidding of the syndicates or facing deadly consequences.

'Some of these guys are loyal employees. But then one day they are suddenly faced with extreme intimidation. Some of these rangers live in the communities around our parks. Their families live there. Then one day the criminals come by. They'll say, oh we see your husband or wife works in the park. We're sure you don't want to see them getting hurt. This is a dangerous country. People are murdered. So we'll give you some money, in exchange for some information. That would be the smart thing to do. If you don't want our money, things might turn out badly for you.'

Unfortunately, the threat is all too real. People in the wildlife industry know that very well, so they comply. Despite all the obstacles they faced, the Hawks had some tangible feedback about the success of Operation Blood Orange.

'SANParks came back to us,' Danie told me. 'And they said that after the arrests of the suspects in Blood Orange, there was a marked decrease in the poaching incidents in the area.'

In fact, there were no incursions for 155 days. 'At the end of the day, that's our goal. We need to make an impact. So that there can be a drastic decrease in poaching incidents.' The state prosecutor on the Blood Orange case is considering adding charges of racketeering to the case, something that Johan hopes will happen.

'Because that's what we want to see at an organised crime level. Because it has a dramatic impact on corruption. When you have that kind of impact inside the park . . . If you can keep the park clean, it makes it that much more difficult for the criminals to get in there.'

It's all part of the bigger picture that the Hawks look at. Danie said another element they use to get at the criminals is to hit them where it hurts most – the money.

'To them it's all about money and power. And of course, their money comes from the proceeds of crime. So then we will come for your money. So we use the Asset Forfeiture Unit and we use the court processes available to us to do that.' This is why, in Project Python, the cash that Huang had paid for the rhino horns was forfeited to the state, along with several vehicles that had been used to transport their illicit goods.

Johan and his team have a motto: Beat them to the exports. But that's much easier said than done. 'Corruption plays a huge part here again,' he said. 'The structures involved in exporting the horns can't exist without some form of corruption. Especially if you look at places like our big ports, OR Tambo International Airport for example. We've put so many things in place to stop them from getting through there. But they want to beat us to the exports. So they'll recruit officials inside the airports. And they've got the money to do it.'

It's massive problem – one Danie remains determined to fix. 'It's a war zone out there. The rhino-poaching statistics are nightmarish. And the truth is South Africa has many rhinos. So we have a duty to protect them.'

Despite their local successes, rhino poaching remains one of the five most lucrative forms of organised crime. So, the final part of the Wildlife Trafficking Unit's job is to deal with the markets in Asia. Johan has spent a lot of time working with his counterparts in the East. It's a strategy he hopes will pay off in the long term.

'The reasons behind them wanting rhino horn might surprise you,' he told me. 'Most people locally think it's used as traditional medicine. And that is a small part of the demand. But what we've seen lately is what we call the Ferrari effect. It's seen as a luxury item. So the horn is used as jewellery, or it's crushed into a powder and drunk in the nightclub scene. Many people believe it will prevent a hangover. And it's expensive. So it's something to show off with. To say look how rich I am, I have access to these products. So it has a lot more to do with bragging rights than medicinal use.'

Part of their efforts to fight the market, Johan told me, was to make use of CITES, the Convention on International Trade in Endangered Species of Wild Fauna and Flora. 'We went so far as to convince CITES to make a resolution that if rhino horns are confiscated in other countries, they should send us samples. That opens up a whole new dimension for us in terms of information management, how the puzzle pieces fit together. Because it's actually a puzzle that you're building.'

Gideon Jones says part of the solution lies in education. 'The smugglers, the people who are dealing in illegal horns, they don't see a rhino as an animal, or a living being. They only see it as a commodity. They won't change. But perhaps the public, the people buying the product, perhaps they could change.'

This is part of the work Johan and the team are doing with their international counterparts. 'The public buys the commodity. But it's a commodity that has no emotional connotation. It's like a piece of wood they buy. But they don't know where the piece of wood comes from. So we've been doing a lot of work to show them that what they're buying is coming from an animal. An animal that was most likely cruelly killed in a place like the Kruger National Park,' he said. It's an ongoing discussion, even with law enforcement on that side of the world. 'For instance, in Singapore, in terms of their law, it was a nature conservation infringement. Which was just penalised with a fine. Now we've offered a different point of view, another way to look at it. We've explained the money-laundering aspects to them. The bigger organised crime picture. And that has changed so many things. So they can now prosecute in terms of other laws, that carry hefty jail time, ten-year sentences and so forth.'

The Hawks have roped in organisations such as Interpol and the UNODC – even United for Wildlife, the organisation founded by Prince William and the Royal Foundation to end wildlife trafficking.

'We have to look at our Southeast Asian countries. And the truth is these were very difficult countries to sit and negotiate with. You're looking at differences in time zones. Language barriers. Cultural differences.' But some of the work has paid off. Recently, the Hawks have been approached by Vietnamese officials, Johan added. 'They asked us if we could help them with our methodologies. Could we explain things to their government departments, to their law enforcement. And we did.' They embarked on a huge information-sharing campaign, one I'm told involved a lot of Vietnamese translations.

'We lived the tragedy that happened over here,' Johan sighed. 'But that allowed us to fine-tune our whole strategy on how to address the scourge. It's not necessary for other countries to go and reinvent the wheel here. They change a few things here and there to suit their laws, but it forms the foundation of how to deal with any syndicates within the broader environmental affairs landscape.'

It's a multipronged approach they hope will pay off. It would be devastating to think that the only place future generations could get to see a rhino would be in the pages of a book.

'I think South Africa,' Johan concluded, 'since we've started to stabilise this tragedy with rhino poaching, has learnt a lesson. Our suffering has given us the ability to show the world that we are the leaders in this field, we can give our skills to our neighbours, we can give it to countries across the world. And I am positive that in the years to come, this is going to have an even bigger impact on wildlife trafficking in general.

I, for one, certainly hope he is right.

6

THE NOT-SO-USUAL SUSPECTS

In April 2014, one of the largest cash heists in South African history took place in the small town of Witbank. It was a daring operation, pulled off with military precision. The armed gang behind the crime managed to get away with more than R100 million in cash. It must have felt like winning the lottery. Especially since they were pretty sure they'd get away with it. How could they not? After all, the policeman assigned to investigate the case was one of their own.

Just a few minutes' drive from the Union Buildings, the official seat of the South African government in the capital city of Pretoria, I found the nondescript brown high-rise I'd been looking for. I was surprised that this was where the GPS had led me. Pretoria is my hometown, and I know its streets very well. I thought I knew most of the buildings the DCPI used as offices. Apparently, I was wrong.

I glanced up the road at the well-manicured lawns that form the base of the Union Buildings. I'd covered some memorable events there, everything from presidential press conferences to Madiba's lying in state.

The imposing sandstone structures, featuring a mixture of neoclassical, Cape Dutch and Edwardian designs, are situated atop Meintjieskop in the suburb of Arcadia. The location offers unrivalled views of the city skyline. Briefly, I wondered if any of the government officials walking those corridors had ever seen R100 million in cash . . .

I'd come here to meet Captain Manie van Zyl and Warrant Officer Paul Holtzhausen from the DPCI's Organised Crime Unit. Both men were attached to the division's Violent Crimes Section. The interior of Holtzhausen's office, where we sat down to discuss the case, came as no surprise. No windows. No views of the city. Drab-coloured walls. An old wooden desk and a few even older-looking chairs took up most of the space. Functional, yes. Anything to write home about? No.

What the office lacked in the looks department was made up for by the friendly welcome I received from the two officers. While they have vastly different physical characteristics, both men had that look about them that I could only describe as the look of seasoned detectives. I don't think either would look out of place in a film noir crime series.

Removing a bulletproof vest from the ageing blue office chair that would soon become my seat, Paul greeted me with a firm handshake. Tall, middle-aged, with a shaved head and a 9mm pistol holstered at his side, the warrant officer made for an imposing figure.

Manie, by contrast, is shorter and stocky, his dark hair cropped short. He sported a neatly cut moustache, highlighting a jawline that seemed as if it was permanently covered in a five o'clock shadow.

'On the 27th of April 2014, I received a call from my provincial head,' Paul kicked off their story. 'He told me he wanted me to go to a crime scene in Witbank, where SBV's cash depot had been robbed of R107 million.'

SBV specialises in securely moving cash, and its clients include some of South Africa's largest banks. They own more than 700 armoured vehicles, have 30 processing facilities and employ about 6 400 staff. The depot in Witbank was used as a secure storage facility, where cash being moved between banks and retail businesses could be stocked.

'I immediately realised this was going to be a big case, and we put together a team that would comprise me as the main investigating officer, Captain Manie van Zyl and Warrant Officer Piet Zeeman.'

Manie's role would be to supervise the investigation and provide much-needed logistical support.

'It was a big case. It was the biggest theft case in South Africa. So I think that's why our provincial commissioner wanted to get the Hawks involved,' Manie said.

Behind every crime, there's a motive. When it comes to organised crime, the overarching motive is always money, from rhino horn smuggling to mafia and drug operations to human trafficking.

'On the day of the robbery, a large gang entered the SBV premises. They overpowered the guards, broke open the safes and made off with the cash, later sharing the spoils,' Manie said.

Where there's this much cash, the risks are enormous, but the paydays are equally big. It's no wonder, then, that in a country where the police force is under threat from an ever-dwindling budget and skyrocketing crime rate, cash-in-transit (CIT) companies like SBV have become targets of organised crime syndicates. According to Anni, the trend is on the increase.

'Between 2014 and 2017, cash-in-transit heists increased by 100 per cent, where there were at times up to five heists in a day,' she told me. Because of a strong police response to the crime, the syndicates also targeted the cash depots where the money was kept. Although these cases are far less frequent, Anni says they also increased in that time. 'These kinds of robberies increased by 200 per cent over the same period.' It is still common to see cash-in-transit heists make the headlines every other week.

'Initially, I'd only gone to pick up the docket. The crime scene had already been processed,' Paul said. The scene had been handled by a detective constable, Khubeka, from the local police station. He'd taken the initial witness statements and overseen the forensic team. At the time, he had no idea that the Hawks would be called in to take the investigations further.

Manie said their initial investigation soon painted a clear picture of how the brazen robbery had been executed.

'A group of about twenty suspects had pulled off the robbery. Most of them got together that day in Sunnyside, Pretoria, where they had to hand in their phones to the ringleaders.'

This was a clever tactic and an early indication that the leaders were running a sophisticated syndicate. Cellphone communications between individuals on the day of the heist could connect them to the crime later.

The leaders also knew that if the police caught one of the gang, his or her phone could lead them to the other crew members. Only a select few, probably the most trusted among them, were handed burner phones. A burner phone is a cellphone that cannot be traced back to you. It would typically have been bought with cash, and the SIM card in it would be registered under a fake name or not registered at all. It wouldn't have your contact list on it either. Burner phones would normally be used to contact the kingpins to update them on the gang's progress or about any problems.

'From there, they travelled to Bronkhorstspruit, where they regrouped at a safe house they were using. There, each of them had their roles clearly spelled out, and a sangoma gave them traditional medicine,' Manie continued.

It is common for criminals to approach traditional healers such as sangomas before attempting their crimes. They'll often ask for muti, traditional medicines, to assist them to succeed in their endeavours or hide from the authorities.

Paul picked up the story, explaining the next steps of the plan. 'They gained access to the depot by first sending in two of the syndicate members disguised as police officers. A male and a female. They arrived there and told the guards on duty that they were busy investigating a case of theft, which had ostensibly been opened against one of the guards.'

Paul would later show me photos of the fake police ID cards the gang had used that he'd kept from the docket. The identity documents had been expertly forged.

'They looked just like original police ID cards,' he told me. 'Their photos were on there; they were in colour.'

Whether they're targeting the armoured vehicles transporting the money or the depots where the cash is stored, the syndicates involved in this often-violent form of organised crime are highly professional. These crimes require months of planning and preparation and are pulled off by highly skilled individuals, often experts in their own unique fields. Anni has met some of the country's most feared CIT robbers through her work in our prisons. 'These are individuals who are characterised by strong personalities. They have to be loyal, dependable and unscrupulous. They have to be very brave and have a lot of self-confidence,' she told me.

Gideon says the syndicates are not usually made up of permanent members, something that makes the authorities' jobs that much harder when trying to track them down. The kingpins will hire the individuals most suited to specific tasks. Often, the men involved in the robbery wouldn't have met each other before the job took place. 'Then the kingpins will incorporate experts, for example, safe cutters, someone who can drive, someone who can work with explosives. Someone who can handle himself with a firearm.' So, based on your skills and your experience in the criminal underworld, you get recruited.

Paul said that, on the evening of the heist, the bogus police were used to open the security doors for the rest of the gang. 'That's how they got access to the place. The guards were out-gunned and overpowered, and the gang immediately headed for the safes.'

Not all of the men were armed, and they didn't have to be. According to Manie, the guards who'd been on duty were soon removed from the scene.

'They were held at gunpoint a few kilometres from the scene in a secluded veld. And the rest of the team started unpacking their tools and breaking open the safes.'

In CCTV footage captured that night, some gang members drive a single-cab bakkie into the premises. Its loading bay is packed to the hilt with various cutting torches, gas tanks and drills. Even a generator.

'Among other things, they also used a core drill,' Paul told me. 'A core drill isn't a small tool. You have to fasten it to the ground and then start drilling. Even so, it took them the whole night.'

The gang had planned the heist so meticulously that they even knew when the guards would have a shift change the following morning. When they realised they wouldn't get into all the safes on time, their comrades jumped into action. They waited outside the houses of the new guards who were coming on duty. The SBV employees were kidnapped at gunpoint when they left their homes for work that morning.

Paul said the hostage situation took a turn for the worse at that point. 'They were brought to the other hostages and were given something to drink there. It was some potent drug cocktail meant to render the guards useless.' Unfortunately, some of them ended up in hospital, suffering life-threatening side effects from the concoction they'd been forced to drink. One man nearly didn't make it.

'It took them the whole night to get into the safes,' Manie said. 'As they got one open, they'd move on to the next. And as each one was opened, the cash had to be packed into their getaway van. It was a Mercedes Sprinter van, and they'd removed all the seats from it at the safe house in Bronkhorstspruit.'

The investigators were later told that the van had been packed from floor to ceiling with the bundles of cash. I don't know if you've been in the back of a Sprinter van, but it's not a small space.

'Once they left, they headed back to the safe house in Bronkhorstspruit,' Manie said. 'But they were nervous. There were too many of them in a residential area. So they moved to Ekangala, what they called Dark City.'

Ekangala is a large township remotely located on the border of Gauteng and Mpumalanga. They'd scored so much money that it later emerged that it took them two whole days to count it. Paul laughed at my surprise at hearing how long it took to count the haul. With a sly smile, he told me to try counting a million rand in cash sometime and to let him know how long it took me. 'There were so many notes that at one point, they sent people out to go and buy money-counting machines to help them get through it all,' he explained.

Interestingly, the kingpins behind crimes like these are rarely part of the actual robberies. They'll be far away, monitoring the situation. That is, up until the point when the money is in their hands, says Gideon.

'When the money is there, you'll find the whole lot of them together, all in one place.'

The cash was divided into bundles and placed on a large table before each member could come and fetch his cut.

'The information was that they had a list,' Manie said, 'and as your name was called, you came and fetched your bundle of cash. How much you got was determined by your role in the heist. Apparently, they also got into quite a fight at one point because some got more than others. But eventually, each one got his share, and then they split up.'

The kingpins, who were some of the last people to be arrested, went on spending sprees of note. They bought mansions, cars, Harley-Davidson motorcycles. Paul says they were living it up: 'The one guy bought taxis. He wanted to start a taxi business. Double-storey houses. They went big.'

It's not just about living it up. I've met criminals, some of the bigger players in the illicit gold world, for instance, who have had so much cash lying around that they say some of it eventually grew mould. Believe it or not, getting rid of huge amounts of cash becomes quite a headache for criminals. You can't deposit it into your bank account. How would you explain the transaction? Having millions lying around your home poses a huge security risk. Being a criminal doesn't mean you can't also become a victim of one, especially in the South African underworld. You also can't typically walk into your local supercar dealership, drop R4 million in cash onto somebody's desk and not expect them to ask questions.

But there are always ways of laundering your money, especially if you know the right people. Converting your cash to assets is one way to eliminate the headache.

During his time as the head of undercover operations for the SAPS, Gideon dealt with many organised crime cases. 'In organised crime, if you go and study the underworld, there are always two requirements for the syndicates to operate successfully in cases like these. How do they know where the money is, and how do they know how to steal that money?' he asked me. 'Now, if you were planning this heist, there are only two ways of getting that information. The first is through surveillance. You could, for example, stake out a place, like a house robber watching your home. And the second is inside information. In other words, you have an insider, giving you the info from the inside.'

He said that there would almost certainly have been a combination of the two in big heists like the one in Witbank. You would always need an insider in a secure facility like a cash depot.

'What crime syndicates often do is they recruit someone on the inside. A key member of the staff,' Gideon told me. 'Someone who could pose a major risk to the whole heist. Then they'll recruit that person. They'll approach them and offer them a huge amount of money.' He said greed usually trumps morality, and the insider is quickly won over. 'And where they don't want to cooperate, they'll often be threatened. It's as simple as that.'

From the outset, the Hawks' team knew an insider had to exist. The investigators brought in several staff members they suspected for questioning.

'One of the people we brought in was a woman whose job it was to monitor the alarms. We brought her in with her fiancé,' Paul said. The couple were Gift Nkosi and Jimmy Bouwer. Under intense questioning, they broke down and spilled the beans. 'They came out with the truth. And they told us that they were involved.'

Gift's job was to phone the guards if an alarm was triggered at the facility. 'There was a control room in Johannesburg as well,' Manie recalled. 'So if an alarm went off, the control room would have phoned her. And then she would have said okay, hold on, and she would then phone the guards. The guards – who were, of course, being held at gunpoint that night – just said yes, everything's okay, and she reported that back to the control room.'

This was all just an act on Gift's part, an elaborate smoke-screen she'd hoped would help convince investigators of her innocence later on. She'd thought she'd created the perfect alibi.

'The guards were threatened at gunpoint,' Paul said, 'and of course they reported that everything was fine. Later on, they were then given the drug mixture to drink, probably also to prevent them from reporting the crime too soon.'

The heist had been pulled off with military precision, and the gang had left very few clues. So, Gift's information was critical in sending them on the right track. The breakthrough led to the first arrests in the case, a mere five days after the Hawks had started their investigation. Gift and Jimmy were among the first people taken into custody.

'She gave us a third suspect's name, and we picked him up that same day. He led us to his house in Carolina,' Manie said. The team found and seized over a million rand in cash. 'He'd hidden it in and around his house. Some of it was in a big blue steel toolbox, the rest in a broken washing machine.'

After the arrests, the team met to discuss the way forward with the investigation. Gift's information had only got them so far. She didn't know who the kingpins were behind the heist. This is a typical strategy employed by sophisticated criminals. Information is compartmentalised and only shared on a need-to-know basis. Again, it's an effective way to keep law enforcement from uncovering all the role players.

'So we decided to use two of the people we'd arrested as state witnesses, hoping it would take the investigation forward,' Paul said.

Who knows the most about a crime that has been committed? The investigating officer? The victim? Or the perpetrator? The criminal. Offering an accused the opportunity to receive a reduced sentence or complete immunity from prosecution by turning them into a state witness is an effective tool. In this case, it was a no-brainer for the Hawks. They had very little else to work with.

'That's when you must rely on your section 204 witnesses to get somewhere,' Paul said. State or 204 witnesses get their name from section 204 of the Criminal Procedure Act. The 204 witnesses will have to testify to their crimes in court, and the judge will expect a full and honest account if they hope to escape prosecution.

'The 204 witness Gift Nkosi was very useful. She gave us dates and locations where they'd met. And then by looking at cellphone data, we could see who had attended these meetings,' Manie said.

This was crucial evidence. Analysis of the records backed up what Gift had said in her statements and allowed the Hawks to place certain suspects at certain locations at certain times. It's hard for a criminal to argue in court that he wasn't at a critical meeting when his cellphone places him at the scene in the time frame described by witnesses.

The information soon led to more arrests.

'So we could place certain people at the crime scene on a particular night. We could place them at the safe house where the money was counted.'

This is a classic example of how a decent investigation unfolds. Somewhere along the line, you pick up the smallest tidbit of information. And it points you in a particular direction. That's where you start scratching until you unearth the next clue, and the next. A criminal conspiracy is nothing other than a finely woven web of deceit. But to unravel the web, you need at least one small thread to start picking at.

'The cash we managed to seize also became important evidence in the case,' Paul said. This may sound obvious, but there's more to it than you might think. Keep in mind that the police need to be able to connect any piece of physical evidence they find to the scene of the crime. A suspect found with cash on their person is just that – someone in possession of cash. It doesn't mean they are guilty of anything. In a court of law, the state must prove beyond a reasonable doubt that a given object comes from a given scene.

'In between some of the bills,' Paul continued, 'we found torn pieces of paper. It turned out that these were fragments of labels that SBV used to mark different bundles and denominations.'

The Hawks could prove that the labels came from SBV with forensic analysis. They were printed on identical paper, and the ink matched.

'I think Gift realised the case against her was very strong, as did Bouwer and the rest of the people we'd arrested in the beginning,' Manie told me. 'And the truth is we wouldn't have gotten much further without her testimony because there were police members involved. They were on the scene.'

It's the kind of thing that makes Gideon want to go through the roof. 'It's a disease that is, unfortunately, endemic,' he sighed. 'And not only in South Africa. Because the police, through the very nature of their work, become valuable assets to the people behind organised crime.'

As the Hawks continued their investigation, they realised that the very man who had originally been sent to investigate the case was involved.

'He was Detective Constable Thamsanqa Khubeka, who was from the Witbank detective branch. He was the first policeman on the scene. He'd been on assigned standby duty that day. And the gang had also planned it that way,' Paul said.

The Witbank heist had been carefully planned for a whole year. In their investigation, the Hawks learnt that the robbery would have taken place a week earlier than it eventually did.

'But because Khubeka wasn't on duty that specific weekend, the syndicate had decided to delay their attempt for another week. They wanted him to respond to the scene and handle the docket,' Paul muttered wryly.

That could have meant the end of any real investigation into the heist. As the investigating officer, Khubeka would have been able to manipulate the case, tamper with evidence and cherry-pick the information he put into the docket. Unfortunately for the detective-turned-heist instigator, the Hawks ultimately ended up with the docket. Khubeka was one of the most valuable nuggets of information that had come from the state witness deal with Gift Nkosi.

'Gift used to be a police reservist at Witbank station,' Manie joined the dots. 'That's where she and Khubeka got to know each other. And later when she got the job at SBV, he approached her. He lured her in, asking her for her help with the alarms. And she fell for it.'

Looking at the case all these years later, one can't help but be impressed at the level of planning that had gone into the heist. On paper, it must have been the perfect plan. The fake cops provided the access. They had inside knowledge and assistance during the theft, and they had the actual police investigating officer to cover their tracks afterwards. And if it wasn't for the screw-up with the drug mixture they'd given the guards, no one would have been hurt. If it wasn't for a provincial commissioner in the DPCI's decision to send out a team, they may have got away with it.

The investigation was running smoothly but they still didn't have the mastermind. 'We eventually arrested the two suspects, the male and female, who had initially gained the gang access by pretending to be police, in East London,' Paul told me. 'They were brought up to Middelburg.'

The arrests would prove to be the final nail in the gang's coffin. The female was made a section 204 witness. Both Paul and Manie asked me not to name her, as threats had been made on her life during the trial. She had in fact been placed in witness protection soon after her arrest and remained there until the trial was completed.

As I've mentioned, it's not uncommon for the individuals in these cases not to know each other. The term for this is operational security. Let's say, for instance, you have three groups of people involved in your heist. Suppose the police have a state witness to testify against group one. That keeps groups two and three off the hook. The 204 witnesses can't testify against them. They don't know who the people are or what their roles are. But this specific state witness, whom we'll call Ms London, led the investigators to the very top of the syndicate.

'Her fiancé was a man named Robert Clack,' Paul said. 'We later discovered that he had previously been involved in a cash-in-transit heist. He'd been charged for it, but the case against him was eventually withdrawn.' Interestingly, in this previous case, the guards had also been given drugged drinks. 'And through that case, he had met and befriended another one of the robbers we arrested in this case, a man named Enock Khumalo. And ja, that's how they decided that he and his fiancé would get access to the depot.'

Manie told me they spent hours with Ms London, questioning her and taking her through photographic ID parades of their suspects. She proved invaluable, putting names to faces and filling the detectives in on who played what roles during the heist.

But what they found out from her next would come as a huge shock for both investigators. The man she fingered as the kingpin had been one of their own.

'She gave us a lot of information, much of it unknown to us at the time. And eventually, she gave us the kingpin, a man who used to be in the Hawks. She pointed him out in one of the photographic ID parades we held with her. The former captain Bhekani Welcome Gcabashe,' Paul said.

Many parallels can be drawn between the opposing sides in the case. Just like the heist required a group of experts in their individual fields, brave men who could be trusted to stay loyal and get the job done, the same can be said of a specialist police unit like the Hawks. And suddenly, they were confronted with a former member who was corrupt.

'Ms London had always said it must be a police officer,' Manie recalled from questioning their star witness. She'd met the kingpin but didn't have a name. 'She believed he was because of his body language, the way he spoke. And then his name came up while we looked through cellphone records...'

The 50-year-old Gcabashe had resigned from the Hawks before the heist. He'd been working for a security company that looked after the interests of several mines in the Witbank area.

Here's another scary truth about organised crime, and I can guarantee you it's a phenomenon you will find all over the world. Without corruption, often the kind that involves government employees such as the police, organised crime cannot take place.

'After we found out that Gcabashe might be involved, and he was positively identified in the photographic lineup, we also requested his cellphone records,' Manie said. 'And we could see a lot of communication between Khubeka and Gcabashe. And on the day the 204 witness had told us she'd seen him, the second day that they had counted the money, we could place his cellphone at the scene at the time she had given us.'

According to evidence that eventually emerged in court, Gcabashe had received R40 million as his share of the proceeds from the heist.

'The boss takes his cut,' Gideon would later tell me in one of his typically dry bons mots, 'and he usually takes it first.'

'In court, it was quite apparent,' Manie said, 'that Khubeka and Gcabashe were the kingpins behind the heist.' Their backgrounds in law enforcement certainly played a huge role in the heist's success. 'They knew exactly how to gain entry into the depot: by using the fake police officers. Their planning had been meticulous. It was the kind of strategy that someone who knows how to pull off a robbery would come up with.'

'At the end of the day,' Paul said, 'you don't know who to trust any more. You don't know if the guy next to you might be involved.'

Manie knew Gcabashe quite well. 'I'd worked with him for many years. We were friends. It was really disturbing to me when we realised he was involved,' he said, pensively. 'We'd worked together closely in the past. Our lives had been in danger together, so yeah . . . But if someone crosses the line, they've crossed the line. You can't come back.'

Gideon had similar experiences during his career. I wanted to know what it felt like. 'I think once you realise your colleague is involved in crime, then your whole attitude towards them changes,' he told me. 'You withdraw from that friendship. And it's a pity, it doesn't feel good. In fact, you lose a little bit of your trust in humanity. That's probably why so many detectives are so cynical.'

Despite their successes in the investigation, the case soon took a dark turn for the team of detectives. It's another sinister and common phenomenon when dealing with organised crime. And it reminds me of a symbolic message you'll find references to if you delve into the history of syndicates. It typically involves the recipient receiving a sealed envelope or similar container. Inside, there'll be a bullet and a coin. The implied message is simple: The money, or a bullet to the head. Play along and perhaps even get paid for it or die if you're against us.

'During the investigation, we received death threats,' the Hawks explained. 'We were told that we would be taken out if we didn't discontinue our investigations.'

Manie says they had to take the threats seriously. 'They sent us messages about family members, they knew where we lived. They also told us that we'd end up like our provincial head at the time, who had been shot at his home in an unrelated incident.'

In South Africa, police are often targeted by criminals. But would the syndicate go from robbing a cash depot to murdering the police investigating them? It's hard to tell, but a rather disheartening thought about our justice system is brought to mind. When it comes to serious crimes like the heist, the accused face equally serious jail time if convicted. So, what's to stop them from adding murder to their charge sheet?

Anni told me we'd all like to think we could stand up to threats of this nature if we were in those shoes, but it's not always that easy. 'Many people, depending on their personalities and character traits, will give in once their family members are threatened, especially if it's their children. It's as simple as that.'

One can only imagine that in this case, where so much was on the line for the syndicate, it must have been nerve-wracking to hold out against the threats. But the team didn't give up. They took extra precautions, like moving their base of operations to a clandestine location.

Paul shrugged the incidents off, saying, 'We didn't let it get to us. We were there to do our work, solve the crime, and get everyone involved in court. And as we continued, the threats came to an end.'

By February 2015, the team had arrested all their suspects. In total, sixteen people were caught in the dragnet, of whom three became state witnesses.

'It was hard work, difficult work . . .' Manie reflected. 'But we ended up catching sixteen of them. And I do believe we got the leaders of the syndicate.'

But catching the criminals is only one part of the job. The investigating officer on a case will have to see it through in court. In complex cases like these, that could take a while.

'The case took four years to complete. We called about 206 witnesses.'

Unfortunately for investigators, but often more so for victims, the wheels of the justice system do turn very slowly. I've reported on cases that have run for much longer. Court procedures aside, criminals will, of course, do their utmost to delay their trials. The longer they can delay, the higher the chances that witnesses forget key facts or even pass away. There may be attempts to extort them or pay them off. Anything is possible. In this case, the state prosecutors could put solid arguments forward. The Hawks' docket they were working from was bulletproof.

'Gcabashe argued a lot about where he was,' Manie told me. 'But the proof was there. The experts could prove his phone was there. And it was a mistake on his part to make phone calls at the scene. But he did. And then we had the 204 witnesses who corroborated that, who could testify to his presence. Even the times corresponded. His cellphone was there when she [Ms London] said he was at the house to collect his money.'

Ultimately, all thirteen accused were found guilty on charges ranging from armed robbery and attempted murder to kidnapping. Bhekane Welcome Gcabashe and Detective Constable Thamsanqa Gladstone Khubeka were among them. All 13 accused received 43 years' imprisonment, of which they must effectively serve 20 years. The three state witnesses, including Gift Nkosi, were acquitted. They would not have to serve any time.

'At the end of the day, we seized about R10 million in cash,' Paul said. 'But we took it a step further, and we seized their assets with the NPA and Asset Forfeiture Unit. Houses, motorcycles, cars, taxis. In total, more than R68 million worth of assets were seized.'

The last time I left the two men's offices, I drove up to the Union Buildings. I strolled along the top of the gardens, enjoying the late-afternoon sun and a cup of surprisingly good takeaway coffee I'd grabbed. It was the first time I'd been up there in a non-work-related capacity for a while.

I had a good view of Sunnyside from up there, the place where the gang had first gathered on the day of the heist. The suburb's streets were crowded. Impatient drivers hooted on the gridlocked streets as thousands went about their daily lives, many heading out of the city on their way home.

I wondered how many would ever see R100 000 in cash, let alone R107 million – few, in a country with some of the highest unemployment rates in the world. Unless one of them stumbled on to a secret stash hidden by one of the heist's members . . .

At the time, I'd laughed at the thought. But today, I'm not so sure. The police seized about R78 million in currency and assets. The rest has never been found.

7

BOOBY-TRAPS, EXPLOSIVES AND THE UNDERGROUND WAR

It's funny how life sometimes takes you in circles. I'm not talking about that feeling you get when you're stuck in a rut. This is something completely different. I've often found myself inexorably drawn to certain stories during my journalism career. Certain themes. The choice was rarely a conscious one. Stories ended up on my desk, and I investigated.

The same towns or suburbs also habitually show up, albeit on different stories. Certain characters, too. From lawyers to gangsters, scammers to private investigators, some people repeatedly pop up. It's as if there is some yet-to-be-discovered force at play. A strangely coincidental form of magnetism or gravity. Perhaps it's just some great cosmic joke. If that is the case, I'm yet to see the punchline. I'm not superstitious, but I believe there are some things in life we simply don't have the explanations for.

The small mining town of Welkom is one of those places. As is the gold that the close-knit Free State community is famous for.

During one memorable investigation, we were trying to expose a massive tax fraud that was one of the key drivers of illicit gold smuggling. The complex scam involved making illegal gold legit by creating fake paper trails and claiming VAT on the now-legitimised gold.

We'd been told that one of the kingpins behind this scheme was so rich and powerful that his tentacles had spread to all ordinary citizens in the small town of Springs on the East Rand. He had allegedly corrupted police, magistrates and politicians. We had documentary evidence to prove that he'd traded in more than R1 billion of gold over just twelve months . . .

As part of the story, we wanted to show how the kingpin's operations had corrupted even the pillars of society. We'd been told that the principal of a well-known school in the area was working with the kingpin. One of our sources told us that if we phoned the principal and told him we had gold to sell, he would buy it from us. We decided to give it a try and record the call.

During the conversation, I would play the part of the seller. But I needed a plausible backstory. Our source came up with a credible cover. He told me to tell the principal I was from Welkom and that I could get gold from the mines in the area. 'Everyone in Welkom deals with gold . . . ' was his simple explanation.

The recordings were later broadcast on national television. Believe it or not, the principal was willing to buy a kilogram or two of gold from us based on a few phone calls. At today's prices, that would be worth more than R1 million.

Unbelievably, he wanted us to drop off the gold at his school during school hours.

A month or two after the story went out, we were invited by the Hawks to accompany them on a massive raid they were to conduct on illicit gold smugglers. Where would it take place? Welkom.

The call came from out of the blue. I'd never dealt with the DPCI at the time, aside from approaching their spokesperson for comment on various stories. Journalists aren't often offered these kinds of opportunities by the Hawks.

Either way, we spent a memorable night on a raid that targeted more than 200 individuals, all allegedly involved in the illicit gold trade. The Hawks had completed their investigations into the suspects months in advance and obtained arrest warrants for all of them. The takedown ran from midnight to late the following day. All but a few of the suspects were nabbed.

In the years since then, Welkom has popped up several more times. So, I wasn't surprised when I found out that the gold story I wanted to cover for this book had played itself out in the same town.

'Truth, like gold,' Tolstoy once wrote, 'is to be obtained not by its growth but by washing away from it all that is not gold.' On a freezing winter's morning in Welkom, I found myself smiling at the ironically literal definition that Tolstoy's words had taken on for me.

In the 1950s, the newly discovered Free State goldfields were some of the richest in the world. Situated in the heart of this newfound wealth, the town experienced a dramatic boom. But by the late 1980s, the gold rush was all but over. As the precious underground seams petered out, so did all but a few of the mining operations.

Many people don't realise how much towns like these depend on the mines that operate close by. When those mines went in search of riches elsewhere, Welkom's economy all but collapsed. It was a jobs bloodbath that ran into the hundreds of thousands. Once-flourishing businesses closed their doors, the rot began to set in.

Today, the town is a shadow of its former self and, on many economic indicators, one of the worst-performing urban areas in the country. In the dead of winter, it also gets pretty damn cold over there. Trust me.

The case I'd come here for was an excellent example of how cooperation between law enforcement and the private security sector could impact the fight against crime, so I'd arranged to meet members of the Hawks and mine security.

Ernie van Rensburg spent 25 years in the SAPS. During his tenure, he was the commanding officer of the Gold and Diamonds branch in Welkom. After retiring from law enforcement, the jovial Free Stater joined a private security company. Today, he manages security for Harmony Gold in the area.

Captain Karin du Plessis, from the DPCI's Serious Organised Crimes Unit, also has decades of experience in law enforcement. The curly-haired, blonde detective specialises in cases involving precious metals. Once we got to know each other a little better, we realised that she was part of the Hawks' team that had been investigating the gold kingpin we'd exposed in Springs all those years ago. See what I mean about life and circles?

We met at Ernie's base of operations, a set of single-storey, brown brick offices in a desolate corner of the mine's operations. Mining may bring in big bucks, but it's not pretty. Surrounded by huge waste dumps and endless kilometres of relatively barren land, I'd got lost trying to find it.

'We like the place,' Ernie told me when I arrived at the offices. 'It's out of sight of prying eyes. And we can get our work done here.'

He and Karin took me on a brief tour before we got started. The horseshoe-shaped building housed a control room plastered with monitors displaying CCTV footage, and two-way radios. From there, it was a set of admin offices, a kitchen and a coffee break room, ending in a large boardroom they'd set up to brief me.

The boardroom was covered in large whiteboards where Ernie and his team had visually mapped out the cases they were working on, often in brightly coloured markers. I saw case numbers, images of suspects, notes about vehicles and meetings that were under surveillance.

'The illegal gold industry is an evil in the Free State,' Ernie began. 'When I started here in the early 2000s, we were at the peak of dealing with illegal miners both underground and above.'

It is a national problem and probably one of the country's most lucrative organised crime operations. SARS estimates that the illicit trade costs the economy about R100 billion in lost revenue annually. In my experience, the illegal gold trade is one of the biggest problems, right up there next to the illicit tobacco trade. In fact, these two are often interlinked.

'It's become one of our biggest crime and social problems of modern times,' Karin chimed in. 'In this specific case, I used the word hijacked. Because that is what this syndicate did, they took the Masimong mine, infiltrated it, took over and started a reign of terror. And robbed the mine blind in the process.'

In the Free State goldfields (as in many other parts of the country), the closure of several mines led to massive unemployment. For some of the miners who lost their jobs, turning back to what they knew best was a way out of a life of poverty. They became some of the men we now refer to as zama zamas, people who go underground in mines that are often defunct, searching for leftover gold. Working in some of the most squalid and dangerous conditions imaginable, these men often spend weeks underground, digging for gold with only the most rudimentary tools.

'There's a lot of violence involved and a lot of corruption,' Anni told me. And she's right.

As with so many aspects of South African society, the zama problem is complex. It may seem like a relatively harmless crime. Why not let men enter abandoned mines and dig for leftover gold? They're obviously capable of doing it. But here are two of the many issues that this would create.

The first is safety. Under the best conditions, mining is a notoriously dangerous occupation. Unregulated mining often leads to disaster down below. I've managed to convince zamas to take me underground on several occasions. I wanted to see how they work. To my horror, in many instances, they were finding gold in areas of rock known as columns or pillars. In layperson's terms, the pillars are areas in the gold seams where the mining companies don't mine, dig or blast. They're specifically left in place to help provide structural integrity for the underground shafts and tunnels. They're often still full of gold-bearing material and an easy target for the zamas. But how would you feel if we were a kilometre (often much deeper) underground, and I started kicking over the support columns holding up millions of cubic metres of rock and sand above our heads? That's essentially what they're doing.

The dangers underground can be found around every twisting corner. For example, 31 zamas were killed in an underground methane gas explosion in Welkom in July 2023. In an incident in Klerksdorp last year, a similar number of men died from underground methane gas poisoning.

'They call it blood money,' Anni told me, 'because the zamas earn their money through blood, sweat and tears.'

The second issue is the wave of organised crime that has become synonymous with illegal mining. It didn't take long for well-organised and brutally violent gangs, often armed to the teeth, to realise that illicit gold could be a lucrative source of income. Reminiscent of the Italian mob, the gangs started running extortion rackets on the zamas, offering 'protection' in return for ever-increasing shares of the profits. They bribed police and waged war against rival zamas, resulting in deadly underground shootouts. They opened profitable smuggling routes and devised ingenious plans to launder the gold into the legitimate market.

Today, it's common to find abandoned mine shafts 'owned' by different gangs. Zamas must pay for the privilege if they want to work the shaft. It's an extremely dangerous and difficult crime to try to police. The gangs have 'security' guards stationed at the entrances to the shaft. The men are often armed with assault rifles like AK-47s. They see the police coming from miles away and warn the zamas. The zamas know the underground networks of tunnels and shafts like the backs of their hands, and they can easily disappear down the complex mazes if the police tried to follow them. They also often leave deadly booby-traps to slow the authorities down.

The sad truth for many of the zamas is that they are not the people earning the big bucks since the crime syndicates have taken over.

'The illegal gold often leaves our shores as legal gold, and it's exported to countries like Dubai. We have a saying: Dubai was built on Africa's gold,' Karin said.

In most of the cases I'd looked at in the past, the zamas targeted abandoned mines. Operational mines pose an altogether different challenge, with stringent security measures and high activity levels – which doesn't mean they don't face illegal mining threats, though. But what astonished me about Karin and Ernie's case was the level of infiltration the syndicate had achieved.

The Masimong mine is one of Harmony's operational mines in the Welkom area. It's only a few minutes' drive out of town and consists of two shafts: Masimong #4 and Masimong #5.

I visited Masimong #4 with Ernie. On the drive in, we were greeted by the usual plethora of massive safety signs you'll find at all mining operations. They're usually printed in bright colours, imploring workers to look after themselves. Modern-day mining is all about rules and regulations. Following safe behaviours is drilled into visitors and employees alike with monotonous regularity.

We parked about a hundred metres from the large concrete tower marking the shaft. Even from this distance, you could hear the deep drone of the massive headgear as it spun, allowing the cage to sink deep underground. The cage is a huge steel lift that miners use to get below ground. I've been down gold mines that are nearly three kilometres deep. Sinking to that level usually involves several stops and can take surprisingly long. You need to disembark and walk for hundreds of metres along underground haulage areas to reach the next shaft, which will take you even deeper. I don't mind going underground, but honestly, it's not my favourite place to be.

'In 2013/14, we had a huge problem with zamas underground at Masimong,' Ernie explained. 'We had different factions fighting each other, and we had an increasing amount of assaults against mining staff. We even had cases where staff had been shot.'

Karin said that to complicate matters, some of the staff were involved with the illegal mining activities. 'The zamas posed a dangerous threat to the miners, but at the same time, some of the miners were helping them. So corruption was a huge problem.' In organised crime cases, money talks. 'So if you're earning a salary of, say, R10 000 a month,' she said, 'and you suddenly get offers of hundreds of thousands of rand you could earn from the syndicate, then you'll fall for it.'

The collusion was increasingly causing problems underground. At depths of up to an astounding 1,8 km, the mine's regular staff were running into the illegal operations of the zamas. Another example of how organised crime cannot occur without corruption: the zamas had to pay mine employees off at every step of the way, to get their own down to the murky depths and to get the precious gold back up to the surface.

Ernie recalled just how bad the situation had become. 'You'd get a case where an employee stumbled across the zamas and was assaulted. Or you'd get the zamas threatening our staff to cooperate in their plans, and assaults would occur if the employees didn't want to cooperate.'

It's a treacherous environment for the police or security officials who need to go underground to address the problems – a difficult enough environment to operate in under normal circumstances, and a thankless task to flush out the zamas who knew the underground so well and had created their own tunnels and hiding spots.

'We found that there were different ethnic groups at play underground. Mozambican and Zimbabwean nationals, many of them illegal immigrants, were being used to do the day-to-day work of the zamas. Then, they had a group of Basothos who were running the security. And they all carried firearms,' Ernie said. 'They're also the men who keep the other zamas in line.'

I'd once accompanied a group of zamas down a shaft in the West Rand. I'm tall, and the cramped tunnel made me feel claustrophobic. About halfway down the shaft, we'd stopped in an open area so I could catch my breath. The cavernous space seemed to be part sleeping quarters and part processing facility. In one dark corner, a man sat hunched over a small crucible, using a gas torch to melt down several gold nuggets. Some of the zamas seemed displeased by the presence of a journalist. I remember asking 'Charles', my contact in the group, if the zamas were armed.

'Would you like to see?'

Before I could answer he'd barked a few orders at the group of men in the chamber with us. As if from nowhere, the zamas produced 9mm pistols, shotguns and a variety of assault rifles. They seemed quite proud to be showing off their arsenal. It was a nerve-wracking experience. One man had a hunting rifle equipped with a scope and kept saying 'sniper' as he showed me the gun. Another, who spoke to me in Shangaan, waved a few sticks of explosives around, and a plastic bag filled with what looked like detonator caps. When I asked Charles to translate, he gave me a broad grin and said: 'He says if the guns don't work, he'll make the place go boom.'

Back in the Masimong case, Ernie said the situation had become so dire that it felt like they were losing control of the mine. 'The cases were heaping up. And we arrested a few individuals, but we weren't really able to flush out the rest of them. We were having successes here and there, we even arrested some of our staff who were aiding them, but it really was just the tip of the iceberg.'

Ernie approached the Hawks to help him tackle the problem. Phase one of the operation started like so many others do, with an intelligence-gathering initiative.

'Our information led us to Lovemore Chaba,' Ernie told me. 'He was identified as the kingpin behind the syndicate at Masimong. We kept the information very close to our chests.'

The team delved into his background, meticulously fleshing out the structure of Chaba's operations. Chaba was an illegal immigrant from Zimbabwe who had come to South Africa to seek his fortune.

'There was this whole hierarchy,' Karin told me. 'He was the leader, and he had a 2IC, there was a guy in charge of the security. Then he had his regular staff, the zamas who were the people mining the gold. And then he had a whole other division responsible for bringing in equipment and foodstuffs.'

The intelligence revealed a disturbing truth, one the investigating team had long suspected. The illegal structure underground had grown increasingly powerful; as the syndicate had grown, its operations underground had expanded. Its activities were becoming more and more organised with every day that passed. It had grown into an organised crime syndicate in the true sense of the word – and had resulted in a parallel structure being formed underground. If the gang's activities weren't stopped, the team ran the risk of having that parallel structure take over the legitimate mine. Karin said it was evident that a multidisciplinary approach would be needed. 'We had good relationships with the mine and security companies. And the only way we were going to break the back of the syndicate was to cooperate.'

Ernie said they started burning the midnight oil. 'Our planning started in January 2014; we needed to choose a path to success selectively.'

I don't envy the team having to come up with a strategy to take on Lovermore Chaba's syndicate. The plan would need to take into account the possibility that scores of people would have to be arrested and processed. They would need to be able to keep them in police custody and prosecute them. The team would most likely encounter violent pushback and would need the capacity to deal with the violence. The whole process would have to be structured to deal with any eventualities.

One of their biggest obstacles in the past had been that Chaba's gang had ample warning when police and security arrived at the mine.

'We needed to come up with a unique strategy,' Ernie said. 'Because when we arrived, they had corrupt mine employees who would warn them underground. They saw us coming, and they'd phone underground on the shaft's own telephone lines. And they'd d warn them, and get paid well for the information of course. They'd say security is on the way, they're about to come down. And it took us time to get down. You'd have to get to the shaft, and then wait for the cage. And by that time they'd already scattered to their madala sites.'

The madala sites, as they're often referred to, are usually older areas underground where mining operations have finished and, for all intents and purposes, been abandoned. They comprised endless tunnels and underground excavations, and were the places the zamas called home.

Lovemore Chaba had succeeded in starting up more than just an organised crime syndicate underground; he'd also become the de facto leader of his own underground community. It was a village, which functioned much like the towns above ground. There is nothing particularly striking about Lovemore's features. He looks like an ordinary middle-aged guy. But in reality, Ernie says, Chaba was a ruthless operator.

'He was behind an absolute reign of terror. And he ruled with an iron fist underground. No one went against him. And he made all the decisions. Nothing came in or went out without his permission.'

I've watched videos in the investigating team's docket that illustrate some of the violence Chaba used to control his men. In one clip, a tightly bound zama was being whipped with a crudely fashioned sjambok. The man's screams were terrible to sit through.

When you cut through the mystique with which organised crime syndicates are so often portrayed in Hollywood blockbusters, they often come down to nothing other than dictatorships – ones that don't bother with any legal or social norms.

'He had his own meeting area underground,' Karin said of Chaba, 'his own sleeping quarters. He had his own bodyguards. He had the choice of the best foods. He had his own television and DVD player. He had tapped into the mine's water supplies and the electricity. And he had created two whole processing areas, with plant stolen from the mine, where the gold was processed.' It seemed he was unstoppable. 'And of course, he had the money. The kind of money that allowed for corruption, the money to pay employees and suck them all into his illegal mining activities.'

Above ground, Chaba had several recruitment officers. If prospective zamas wanted to work for him underground, they had to submit their resumes. They could only enter the syndicate if they'd received the green light from Chaba.

Without even realising it, these zamas were signing up for Chaba's very own form of indentured servitude. They started their life underground in debt. There was a price to be paid to get them underground. They had to pay for the mining equipment they needed. For their food. The whole system was structured to benefit Chaba.

'Chaba would bribe security at the entrance gates to allow them in, or have employees lend their access cards to the zamas to get them through the door,' Ernie said. 'Then they'd join the legitimate miners, and wait for the cage to drop them down to the lower banks. Remember we're talking about thousands of people who go underground in a month. Not everybody knows everyone else.'

But many of them *did* know Lovemore. And they lived in fear of him. Gideon Jones has dealt with his fair share of organised crime kingpins.

'Remember, for a criminal to be successful, he needs to know the system. And he needs to figure out how to outwit the system.' If he hadn't been such a successful policeman, I have the feeling Gideon may have made for a criminal to be reckoned with. He has the unique ability to be able to place himself into the minds of his suspects. 'I think we often underestimate the criminals,' he once said, in between bites of a takeaway lunch we were sharing while researching this story. 'We make the mistake of thinking they don't know how their victims function, or the police or the justice system for that matter. Think about it, the more successful the criminal is, the more he knows. It's the foolish criminal who gets caught quickly.'

When new zamas arrived underground, they'd be brought to Chaba's meeting room. There, he'd assign them their different roles, tell them how they'd be paying back the money they owed him, and give them strict warnings to follow the rules.

Karin told me that Lovemore even had his own dedicated phone line, one that could be dialled using the mine's own extensions. 'He had his own extension. There are many phone lines underground. And he'd bribed someone to tap into the mine's system. It led straight to his sleeping quarters, and only certain individuals knew about this. And so you could phone him from the outside world, or even directly from the shaft. And you could speak to him personally.'

By this time, Lovemore and his cronies had spent nearly two years underground. And under his dictatorship, the criminal enterprise had grown into a state-of-the-art money-making machine.

'They weren't using hand tools as you'd find in many zama operations. They had an industrial plant underground, where crushing and sorting were being done with machines. And then they were smuggling the suvalos up to the surface,' Karin said.

A suvalo is the plastic top of a two-litre bottle of soda that has been filled with a gold-bearing material known as amalgam. It's a term you'll often hear the zamas use. Weighing in at about 30 grams, a suvalo was worth roughly R36 000 at 2023's gold prices.

'They'll bribe the mine workers to smuggle the suvalos to the surface,' Ernie told me. 'So how do they do it? Well, they'll often seal them in condoms and hide them inside their body cavities. On the surface, Chaba's people would take the amalgam to smelting houses, where it would be processed into gold. And that's how they'll end up with a nugget of gold.'

'From there,' Karin said, 'refineries and other syndicates will buy the gold. Those refineries operate under the guise of being legitimate because they have the licenses to refine gold legally. But they aren't buying it legally. The gold comes from zamas and smuggling syndicates across the country.'

I wanted to know what kind of money we were talking about. How much was Chaba making?

'We'll never know exactly how much,' Ernie answered. 'But when we eventually hit them, we found gold-bearing material valued at about R120 million.'

A large part of that would have gone to Chaba, not to the men who'd slaved away to find the gold.

As we stepped outside the offices for a little sun and to share a lunch his team had organised for us, he told me that they'd once caught a zama who had spent five years working underground. 'That's the longest period I've ever heard of; we found and arrested the man right here in Welkom. When we brought him to the surface, he was so sensitive to the light he couldn't open his eyes in direct sunlight.'

Back in the boardroom, the team filled me in on Chaba's right-hand man and chief enforcer.

'The man's name was Godfrey Madiba,' Karin told me. 'He was Chaba's personal bodyguard. But he was also his chief enforcer. He was the one who meted out punishments on the zamas. He decided where and when and how.'

Ernie said he was also the man responsible for many of the assaults that had taken place on employees. 'He carried a gun. He was the guy who went after any of our employees who didn't want to cooperate with the syndicate. He was also in charge of the food supplies.'

This is another fascinating parallel structure you'll find at any of the sites where zamas work underground. Foodstuffs, alcohol and even cigarettes are a precious commodity below ground. Remember that the zamas don't have the luxury of sinking down in electric lifts. They have to make their way through treacherously small tunnels, following often-circuitous routes to find the gold they're after. It could take days to travel in either direction. So, there are whole gangs of criminals who specialise solely in taking food supplies down. Of course, the zamas below ground are charged a premium for this service. I've heard of cases where these rackets are more lucrative than the gold-smuggling operations.

Getting supplies underground in a working mine, where bypassing security and employees causes further difficulties, comes at a high price: some zamas have told me they've paid R350 for a loaf of bread. At Masimong, Chaba also had control of this valuable side of the operations. Madiba was the man who made sure everything ran smoothly.

Karin told me that the couriers used to transport the food parcels at Masimong even had their own unique name. 'The men who were allowed underground to become zama zamas weren't always very good at mining. That's when Lovemore would have them work as couriers. And those couriers were called Quantums.' The name was derived from the model of

Toyota minivans that are often used as taxis in South Africa. 'That's where the term originated. He has to carry a bag of food on his back, and he has to travel to the different levels in the mine. So these guys would be sent from a central place where everything was stored, and they'd have to go sell it to the illegal miners wherever they were working.'

'There are very strict rules underground among the zamas,' Ernie said. 'You don't steal from another zama. You'll be killed.' At Masimong, as I've seen in other parts of the country, the bodies of dead zamas were often wrapped in cloth and sent to the surface. Attached to the grisly package, you'll find a note identifying the zama and the contact details of his relatives.

Violence, Gideon told me, is never far away when you're dealing with organised crime. 'You'll always find violence. It's often used to maintain discipline. In this particular case, you also had this very warped type of discipline. When one of the zamas got out of line, they'd tie him up. They'd plant a firearm on him or explosives. Some kind of contraband. At Masimong, security had two cases where this was done to zamas. They'd had gold dust rubbed into their hair as well. They were bound so tightly that the wire they used had cut into the men's arms. And then they were left near the cage, and the zamas themselves let mine security know where to find them.'

Chaba knew that if mine security found the men in possession of these items, they would be charged. Whichever way you look at it, the tentacles of his organisation had the men working for him trapped in their almost inescapable grips. It's something I've seen often in organised crime stories: the people who come into the organisation at the very bottom level being used simply as commodities. Some of them might make it, moving up in the ranks. Most of them never do. The overwhelming majority will stay low-level, poorly paid individuals. It's a lot like playing the lottery. They are attracted by the grand prize, but few will ever see it.

In many ways, it's just another form of human trafficking, in my opinion. Be that as it may, there is one more unique part to this story that we have to get to before I can tell you the ingenious plan the authorities eventually came up with to stop Chaba in his tracks.

We've touched on some of the difficulties the investigators had to deal with to get to the illegal miners. But one of the most astonishing – and the deadliest – obstacles they faced came in the form of booby-traps. Just like soldiers did in the Vietnam war, the zamas planted explosives along certain sections of the mine, rigged with tripwires and set to go off at the slightest disturbance.

'You have to be ready when you go after them. Remember, they have explosives,' Ernie said. 'They plant booby-traps, improvised explosive devices. So you had to be so careful, for example, if you had to enter a vent regulator.' Vent regulators are large steel pipes that investigators often had to crawl through to get from the operational side of the mine to the zamas' side. 'The worst is you might be entering a brand-new area. You don't know what to expect. It's pitch dark. So the zamas can see you coming, shining your flashlight. And even if it's not booby-trapped, they'll shoot at you. So that was quite dangerous.'

The setting of explosive booby-traps is something unique. You won't often find this modus operandi employed by crime syndicates anywhere else in the world. The multidisciplinary team knew they had to come up with a sound strategy if they were to have any hope of taking on Chaba's operation.

Eventually, they came up with a two-pronged approach, which, I must admit, ended up being equally unique. If they couldn't get to the zamas, they had to get the zamas to come to them.

'The unions gave us their support,' Ernie told me. 'We negotiated with them, and a letter was sent out to all our employees, and we implemented a total food ban on the mine.' The idea was to prevent the zamas from getting fresh food supplies. But to do so effectively, even employees were prohibited from taking any food items underground. 'We had to prevent the mine workers from selling their lunch to the zamas underground. At the same time, we focused mine security's efforts on any routes that could possibly be used to smuggle food items in.'

Eventually, the team hoped, the zamas would have to come to the surface or face starvation.

The second part of the plan was to mobilise a huge contingent of security personnel. 'On the 14th of April, we sent in 70 security guards to cut off every conceivable entrance and exit,' Ernie said. 'We established a JOC [joint operational command] with the Hawks on site. And then, together with the police, we started entering the mine with all our forces.'

The JOC knew that the zamas were mostly operational between two levels of the mine – the 1 750 level (1 750 m underground) and the 1 850 level (1 850 m underground). 'This was the area underground they had the most control over,' Karin recalled. 'Our people were split into two groups. Group one went down to 1 750 and started working their way down to 1 810. And the other group went in at 1 810, working their way up.'

Inevitably, the two sides met underground.

'We ran into them eventually,' Ernie said. 'And a shooting incident erupted. They were shooting at us, and we returned fire. Eventually, they set the whole area alight, setting fire to anything flammable they could get their hands on.'

Fire underground is every miner's worst nightmare. The area was soon filled with noxious smoke, and the operation had to be temporarily halted as firefighting crews were brought in to get the fire under control. This respite gave the zamas yet another chance to make their escape into even deeper areas in the mine.

'After we had the fire under control, we could take control of those areas the zamas had abandoned, and we placed our teams down there to keep the zamas out,' Ernie said. 'At the same time, we were following up on leads, trying to trace them and find their hiding places. It was basically a deadly game of cat and mouse taking place nearly two kilometres underground.'

After seven days, the authorities had their first breakthrough when the first lot of zamas handed themselves over.

'You must remember we had the food ban in place, and these guys were hungry,' Ernie said. 'We had arranged for medical personnel to be on standby in our training centre. So anyone who had injuries, even people who were diabetics, were taken for treatment, even though they were in custody.'

The first group to hand themselves over were found in the cage.

'They were sitting there, looking much thinner than they had,' Ernie laughed. 'And as they came up in the cage we were there and we arrested them.' Lovemore Chaba was among the men in that first group to be arrested. 'In total, we eventually arrested 28 syndicate members, including the ringleaders Chaba and Madiba.'

As the men came to the surface, they were arrested and questioned. The interrogations led to a treasure trove of evidence the Hawks could use in the case against the men.

'We found a lot of documents linking the suspects to the underground activities,' Karin said. 'We even found a digital camera containing images the zamas had taken of themselves underground. This was critical evidence. Remember that we had them in custody now, but we still had to win the case in court.'

Eventually, 21 of the suspects were charged under the Prevention of Organised Crime Act (POCA). But during the ensuing investigation, the Hawks came across evidence linking Chaba's girlfriend, Bongela Makoula, to the syndicate.

'She was actually an employee of the mine. She worked underground as a loco driver,' Ernie said. 'We found evidence that she was involved, and she was also charged as accused number 22. It later emerged that they had an intimate relationship, and she eventually had Chaba's child.'

The team was lucky to have state prosecutor Advocate Johan de Nysschen appointed to the case.

'What an excellent advocate. We met with him, and after going through all our evidence, we decided that we had enough to try and prosecute the case under POCA. During the investigation, we seized more than 4 000 pieces of evidence underground,' Karin told me. 'We found letters the syndicate members had written. Invoices, bank statements. Some of the documents had their names on it. They kept records of how much gold they were handling in notebooks. It showed how much food they bought . . . '

These pieces of evidence were so critical during the trial because many of the suspects denied that they'd ever been underground, much less worked as illegal miners. 'Some of the suspects claimed that they were hunting rabbits on the surface near the shaft. And we supposedly arrested them there and then brought them in,' Ernie said. But the documents – and, even more damningly, the photos the zamas had taken of each other during their months underground – proved the opposite.

'There was no way that you could claim you were never underground or you had been caught on the surface and brought to the mine,' Karin said. 'Because below the surface, the evidence was found that showed you were indeed down there.'

'We were really proud that eventually we had a first-of-its-kind outcome. This was the first time that zamas, who had been caught underground, were successfully prosecuted under the POCA. Above ground is a different story,' Ernie said.

After a long and protracted court battle, 21 syndicate members were found guilty under the POCA. They were found guilty on more than 800 charges, some of which included managing an enterprise that had conducted racketeering and participating in an enterprise that had conducted racketeering. In total, the accused received more than 2 000 years' imprisonment, of which they'll have to serve 456 years effectively. Lovemore Chaba will effectively serve 25 years. Accused number 22, Chaba's girlfriend, was found guilty on charges of money laundering and racketeering.

The Hawks and their public sector partners have maintained their momentum in the Free State, and in the past few years, illegal mining activities in the province have significantly declined.

On a hill outside of town, where we stopped for a final look at Masimong, I asked Karin about the current situation with zamas on the mine.

'We've kept the pressure up,' she answered, 'and many of the syndicates have moved to other provinces, to the North West and to the East and West Rand areas. Masimong has no zama activities at this time.'

8

FOREIGN DELICACIES

There are many ways for organised crime syndicates to make money. We've covered a few of them already. Unfortunately, South Africa, with its wealth of biodiversity, has an abundance of another commodity in high demand by criminal networks – its fauna and flora.

From the illegal trade in rhino horn or lion bones to the smuggling of succulents unique to the Karoo (a relatively new crime, fuelled by illicit international markets, which is having a devastating effect on that beautiful part of the country), it is a sad state of affairs.

I investigated my first, and certainly one of my most memorable, wildlife stories many years ago. It started off when I was contacted by a source who told me that he had in turn been approached by a group of poachers who had live pangolins for sale.

'Pangolins?' I'd asked. 'Why would anyone want Pangolins?' It turned out that the little scaly anteaters are some of the most trafficked mammals in the world. It's estimated that they account for about twenty per cent of all illegal wildlife trade globally. In South Africa, a live specimen is worth upwards of R150 000 on the black market.

Why, you might ask? Because of an almost insatiable international demand for their scales. In many Asian countries, pangolin scales are highly valued for their supposed healing properties, which – just like rhino horn, by the way – have been scientifically proven to be absolute nonsense. In some countries, pangolin meat is also seen as a delicacy. During my research at that time, I was shocked to discover that, in 2017 alone, 34,7 tonnes of pangolin scales had left African shores. That means between 30 000 and 60 000 pangolins would have been killed.

Intrigued, I pitched the story to my editorial team. The plan was to raise awareness about the plight of these creatures that many people seemed to have never heard of and to expose the smugglers who wanted to sell them. What had initially seemed a straightforward story ended up being quite an adventure.

I'd asked the source to tell the smugglers he had a buyer, a businessman from Johannesburg. They agreed, and we set off towards Phalaborwa, where I would pretend to be the businessman. I would be carrying a hidden camera to record everything that transpired. The poachers had told us they had two live pangolins and, to protect the animals, we told them that I would only buy them if they were still alive when we got there.

It was a race against time. Unfortunately, pangolins don't do well in captivity. In most cases they simply don't survive, which is why you won't often get to see them outside of the wild. On the way down, we contacted the Endangered Species unit of the local SAPS and asked them for their assistance on the case.

They agreed, even though it was a tricky situation for them legally, and in the end, they offered to help us by making my source a 252A agent. When we arrived at the Hoedspruit Police Station, the gravity of what we were trying to do sank in.

The captain who would be in charge of the SAPS side of the operation warned us that the syndicates in the area were notoriously dangerous. And most likely armed. But I was determined to get both the footage and the story.

The poachers were holed up at a safe house in a township near Phalaborwa called Lulekani. But they were nervous and didn't want to give us the address before we arrived. That, in turn, made the police nervous. They'd wanted us to lure the poachers out into the open by setting up the meeting on an open piece of road somewhere. It's safer to make arrests out in the open than to have to enter a residential address, not knowing how many people are inside. Or whether they are armed.

What followed was a wild goose chase, as the woman representing the poachers, known only to us as Leah, had us driving around in circles in Lulekani. We later found out that the poachers had been watching us. We'd driven past the safe house several times.

Eventually, Leah met us along the road, climbed into our vehicle and directed us to the safe house. It was just me, our source and a cameraman who was pretending to be my hench-man in the car. The police were waiting at a nearby shopping centre. On arrival at the rather dilapidated-looking house, we were told that we weren't allowed to speak to anyone or use our phones. We would only be allowed to see the pangolins.

It was a tense situation. Several young men were lounging in and around the back of the house, keeping a close eye on us.

We'd been nervous that the poachers could be setting a trap in the hopes of robbing us of the R200 000 in cash they'd demanded for the animals. So, we'd made very sure that they understood we wouldn't have the cash during this first meeting. This had the dual purpose of hopefully keeping us safe and giving us a reason to leave without having to pay for the animals.

The poor creatures were being kept in empty steel cages in a shed at the back of the premises. They had no food or water. And they seemed stressed. We managed to get this all recorded on a hidden camera.

The supposed viewing done, we promised to return as soon as we'd picked up the cash, which we'd told them was being kept nearby. I breathed a sigh of relief as we left the house. So many things could have gone wrong.

We rushed back to the police to let them know what we'd seen and to confirm that they were indeed in possession of two live pangolins. They'd come prepared: along with members of the Limpopo Endangered Species Unit, they'd called in the assistance of a specialised anti-poaching team. The task force was satisfied, and we set off in convoy back to the house. We would point out the location.

There are few things that can get your adrenalin flowing like joining a police raid. As the convoy of about five vehicles entered the yard, armed members of the task force jumped out of the vehicles, ready for anything.

I will never quite forget the look of pure consternation that crossed Leah and the poachers' faces at the sight of police members carrying huge assault rifles entering the yard.

But within seconds, all hell broke loose. A gunshot rang out, shattering the eerie silence that had filled the yard only moments before. At the same time, the poachers decided to make a run for it. Men scattered across the yard, some jumping over the walls to neighbours' houses in an attempt to escape. In the ensuing chaos, the anti-poaching team also opened fire, and the small backyard seemed to turn into a war zone.

Being in the middle of a firefight, as I'm sure anyone who's spent time in the police or army will tell you, is nothing like what you see in the movies. It's pure chaos. The boom of assault rifles is deafeningly loud. Bullets are flying, and you're not even sure who is shooting at whom.

When the dust cleared, the police had arrested five of the poachers and Leah. The highly trained task team had fired mostly warning shots to subdue the men, and no one had been injured. Whoever had shot at us first was long gone.

The poor pangolins had spent the past week in those cages. We got to accompany the police when they took them for a checkup at a local wildlife vet. It turned out that they had no major injuries, and they were later released back into the wild at an undisclosed location. I still have a video clip somewhere of the two unassuming little creatures marching off to their new home under a majestic African sunset.

But this story isn't about pangolins. My foray into the underworld of the illicit wildlife trade had come to mind while I'd been sitting and waiting to meet Warrant Officer Alroe Luiters of the DPCI's Serious Organised Crime Endangered Species Unit. He's also stationed at the old SARS building in Bellville, Cape Town, where I'd previously met Capt. Lizelle Herbst on the human trafficking case. It was still raining in the Cape when I spent a couple of days with him.

For Alroe and the men and women who make up the Endangered Species Unit, many of their days are spent working on abalone (perlemoen) cases. It's a notorious problem in the Western Cape. Abalone is a type of marine snail. The abalone found on the South African coast is unique to the country's waters and is a natural resource that's quite easy to find. And, like pangolins, they're a sought-after delicacy in many Asian markets. The trade in abalone is highly restricted under South African law. But with an almost insatiable international market to supply, it's become a money spinner for organised crime syndicates.

When I first met him, Warrant Officer Luiters was dressed in a black suit, collared white shirt and colourful red tie that complemented his stocky build. Two gold rings adorned the middle and ring fingers of each of his hands. He wore his hair shaved down to the bare minimum, his devil-may-care smile hinting at a playful nature behind his otherwise serious appearance.

'Abalone is a shellfish that you'll find along our east coast as far as East London. Right across to our west coast up to Port Nolloth,' he told me. In Asia, abalone is a prized traditional medicine and often turns up on the tables of fine dining restaurants. 'The flesh is considered an aphrodisiac,' Alroe said. 'And it is a sought-after dish on many menus. It's actually quite an exclusive delicacy and expensive, not just anyone can afford it. The shell is often used to make jewellery with,' he continued, flipping through a thick pack of printed images from his many cases.

Gideon told me the trade is a fertile breeding ground for criminal syndicates: 'The smuggling of abalone in South Africa is connected to both local and international organised crime.

Abalone is just another commodity to them. A commodity that can make money. And obviously, that's where you'll find the organised crime.'

Anni added that, in many cases, abalone wasn't sold only for cash. 'It's quite common to find the syndicates entering into barter agreements,' she said. 'So it's not always money involved. A lot of times they're exporting the abalone to international markets, in exchange for commodities that are in high demand inside our borders. It could be drugs, it could be firearms. Something that those syndicates can offer our underworld.' And the scale of the problem in South Africa has reached epic proportions. 'In 2019, it was estimated that the illegal trade in South Africa was worth a billion rand annually.'

Going into this story, I'd pictured abalone smuggling as a few guys who went out diving along the coast, peeling off the abalone they found on the submerged rocks or inside the kelp forests the sea creatures often call home. But in a high-stakes game like the international abalone trade, where billions are at stake, it becomes organised to the finest degree.

'The Asian syndicates have targeted the poorer communities living along our coastlines,' Alroe told me, 'offering them easy money to exploit our natural resources.' But he says that's had a knock-on effect in those same communities – as the crime syndicates grew, so did other associated problems. 'There's been an increase in drugs, in violent crime, it's filtered through.'

An increase in the drug trade in any area leads to other socioeconomic problems. Theft, home invasions, domestic violence, murders – they're all interlinked.

As law enforcement efforts to address the problem have increased over the years, the masterminds behind the syndicates have been forced to use increasingly devious and often brutal techniques to satisfy the demand. But the rewards far outweigh the risks.

'Abalone is a free product. It doesn't cost you anything to manufacture it. You just need to go and dive it out of the sea,' Alroe explained. 'But if you can land it in Asia, it's worth about R6 000 per kg. You removed it from the sea for free, but you're getting that insane amount for it that side.'

Many of the dreaded Cape gangs have also got involved with the smuggling syndicates, bringing with them even more violence. Anyone who gets in their way is dealt with immediately.

'Because there's so much profit at stake, there's a lot of infighting between the syndicates,' Alroe told me. And he should know. He's seen the violence first-hand. 'It's become increasingly dangerous. I have myself been chased by gang members out of areas while I was busy with investigations. They chased me right until about a kilometre away from the nearest police station. And they were all armed.'

In the Western Cape, gang violence is often the leading cause of murders in the province. Much of that is related to turf wars and power struggles. And, according to the police, the allure of the gangster lifestyle is attracting increasingly younger generations. During a media briefing in August 2023, provincial police commissioner Maj. Gen. Tembekile Phathekile said, 'You can see by the killing of children that young boys are joining gangs and fighting older gangs.'

How the abalone syndicates operate in the Western Cape reads like a masterclass in Organised Crime 101. 'Abalone smuggling happens in three phases,' Anni told me. 'The first phase is the diving operations. The second phase comprises the drying and processing of the product, and the third phase is the distribution to the different markets.'

Phase one starts with the syndicate identifying an area where they can dive for the abalone. This part of the crime is usually carried out by low-ranking members of the organisation. 'They'll operate in groups of anything between five and fifty people,' Alroe told me. 'You'll have the divers, who will go underwater and physically get the abalone. And they'll always have at least one spotter. This guy will be positioned on high ground, keeping his eyes out for the authorities.'

The divers will typically be carrying knives and nets, and at least one will have a phone on him. 'They'll use these small burner phones,' Alroe said. 'And keep them wrapped up in condoms to keep the water out. And that's how they can communicate with the spotters.'

This phase of the operations is notoriously difficult to crack down on. When the authorities arrive, the divers will simply make their getaway underwater. And the spotters won't be found with anything incriminating on them. You can't arrest someone for sitting in a car next to a beach.

Alroe says these crews are often quite arrogant. 'You'll arrive on the scene, shouting police, police. And they'll be swearing at us, showing us middle fingers, and then they'll disappear under the water and head out towards the open ocean. They don't care, they have no respect for authority.'

The divers will be assisted by other low-ranking members of the syndicate who stay on shore, known as carriers. Their only function is to serve as pack mules. They'll carry the bags of abalone into a secluded area nearby.

'That's when the driver comes in,' Alroe said, twisting one of his rings back into a forward-facing position. 'Or I should say the first driver. They're clever. The low-ranking guys don't know where the processing facilities are. So they'll use multiple drivers.'

The warrant officer says he's tailed many a driver, only to find that they've stopped at a petrol station or takeaway joint, for instance. 'So the driver will stop there and leave the abalone in the car. And he'll leave the keys in the car or perhaps put them on one of the vehicle's tyres. And then he'll go and wait inside, maybe order a burger or a coffee.'

Another person, one usually higher up in the syndicate's ranks, will then arrive and drive the car to the processing facility. 'He'll go and drop the abalone off, and then he'll return to that same takeaway place, and leave the vehicle there again, and walk away. And then the guy inside will come out, get into the vehicle, and drive off.'

In most instances, the two drivers will not even know each other, a clever way of compartmentalising the syndicate's operations. Should Mr A be caught, he can't betray Mr B. It's also a security measure put in place to protect themselves from rival gangs. Only a few of the most trusted members will know the locations of the processing facilities, where millions of rands of stock are stored.

'But that's not all,' Alroe told me when I'd asked if that was pretty much it for phase one. 'From the moment that the abalone leaves the ocean, it will be monitored. This will be done by some of the syndicate's most trusted, and often most feared, members.'

The kingpins have a lot invested in these shipments. And a lot to fear. Between the police, rival gangs and possible enemies within their ranks, they can't be too careful.

'So they'll always have eyes on their products. So just as we try and have effective surveillance on them, they come in with their counter-surveillance methods.'

Phase two of their operations starts when the abalone arrives at their processing facilities. These facilities range in size from industrial-grade warehouses to homes rented in affluent suburbs. The only real requirement is that, when the facilities are viewed from the outside, no one should be any the wiser.

'They want to operate in the shadows. They don't want to draw attention to themselves. Some seem to think a suburban home offers a great disguise, while others will use factories. I've found processing facilities all over Cape Town. In the wealthiest areas and the poorest.'

Every syndicate has its unique recipe, but in general, the processing involves removing the fleshy feet from the shells, after which they're washed, boiled, and finally dried.

'Inside these facilities, we usually find salt, chemicals and propane gas tanks used for heating. And the smell. The smell is something unique, and the processing plants are usually not very well ventilated to keep the smell from reaching the outside world.'

Alroe told me that during their raids, the police would break out in a sweat just a few seconds after entering these kinds of premises. The heat generated from the cooking and drying is intense.

'I can't believe that the syndicate members work in those conditions. They'll often live right there as well. Right next to a room packed with industrial-size steel drying racks, you'll find the guy's bed.' Picture living in a heated sauna that reeks of fermented fish, and you'll get the idea.

It takes about a week to dry out a batch of abalone flesh. Once that's done, each piece is weighed and graded. The grading will, of course, determine the price.

'The better it is, the more it is worth,' Alroe said. 'Often when you seize a load, you'll find the boxes that the abalone have been packaged in have been marked. The marking will denote the grading, A being the best and biggest specimens, right down to C and D grades.'

Phase three entails smuggling the product out of the country. 'There isn't any significant market for abalone locally,' Gideon said. 'They have to get it out of the country. That's where the big money is.' As with any large cross-border smuggling route, the abalone can be transported by land, sea, or air.

Alroe told me that the Hawks focused on the second and third phases of the operations. That's where they could have the most significant impact on the syndicates and where the senior members of the syndicates could be most often found. 'It's common to see them transport the abalone by road, in trucks or trailers. It will be hidden in secret compartments, or stashed in between other goods. The trucks will then bribe their way across the borders to neighbouring countries. Many of these don't have the same strict import and export controls you'll find in South Africa. So from there, they'll just load it on a plane to its end destination,' he said.

It will all depend on the specific syndicate, and their capabilities to move the product clandestinely. This is also the phase where you'll find the most corruption.

During the short break we took while Alroe attended to some official business, I had time to study the newspaper clippings that adorn his office walls. The headlines were telling.

'Officials appear over poaching of abalone', read one *Cape Argus* report. Another that appeared in the *Hermanus Times* in 2018 led with 'Hawks swoop on syndicates', with the opening lines of the article reading: 'Nine Fisheries Control Officers tasked with protecting marine resources appeared in court yesterday . . . '

I've said it before: there is no way for organised crime to thrive without corruption. It's as simple as that – a symbiotic relationship.

One of the most effective ways to combat the sophisticated nature of organised crime is through effective intelligence gathering. The Hawks rely on information gathered by the SAPS Crime Intelligence, and they have agents and confidential informants inside crime syndicates too.

'It's a difficult world to try and gather sources from,' Anni told me. 'Keep in mind that just like with other forms of organised crime, say human trafficking for instance, it's all about exploitation for the syndicates.' They'll specifically recruit members from poverty-stricken communities along the coast, exploiting factors such as high unemployment, drug and alcohol addiction, and broken homes. 'Many of the syndicate members will be the only breadwinner in a home, they might be the sole source of income for a whole family,' she said. 'And of course, they spend their money in the communities. They bring money and power and wealth. So getting one of their own to turn on them is not the easiest thing.'

But when they do receive intelligence, they have to act. And they don't always have the luxury of weeks to plan a takedown operation. Sometimes the information is about an imminent event, and officers like Alroe simply have to respond immediately.

Outside Alroe's office, the grey Cape sky cast ever-darkening shadows across the buildings, and the wind lashed the rain against old windows that could have done with a good wash. Later that day, my splendid view of Table Mountain from the guest house I was staying at would have vanished behind the thick masses of clouds.

'On the 17th of May 2021, I got a call from my commanding officer,' he told me. His commander had received information from a confidential informant about a truck that may have been transporting abalone. 'I was driving along the N1 highway at the time. The truck was reportedly on the N7. So I headed in that direction.'

On his way, he hurriedly liaised with fellow law enforcement officials from the Department of Agriculture, Forestry and Fisheries, Crime Intelligence, and fellow Hawks' officers. 'And we picked up the truck in the Panorama area. It had a foreign registration number. And it was a big white delivery truck, the kind that has the big steel doors at the end.'

The task force that had been hastily assembled decided to hang back at first and keep the truck under surveillance. None of the officers were in marked police cars.

'We realised that a white Audi was driving suspiciously near the truck as if they were in convoy. I've worked on abalone cases since 2013, and by now I know when I spot them. You can just tell from how they're moving – the drivers of both vehicles are on their phones at the same time, talking to each other.'

As the surveillance continued, there was no doubt in the minds of the officers following the pair of vehicles that they were working together. They seemed glued together, never wandering very far from one another.

'It was a two-litre Audi, and he was driving along the highway at 60 km/h. Why else would he do that? Then he was in front of the truck, then behind it, but always near it.'

There's quite an art to following another vehicle without being seen. Especially if the vehicle is being driven by a criminal. They're always on the lookout for any threats. It's not as easy as you might think. Especially not when a secondary or pilot car is involved. Usually, it's the people in the pilot car's specific role to keep an eye out for the cops.

'Our cars weren't marked. And we were rotating. So one car would be behind them, and then we'd switch so that another would be following,' Alroe told me.

When trained agents in multiple vehicles are keeping you under surveillance, you'd be hard-pressed to spot them. If they have enough cars, especially on a highway like the case was that day, they can even have one of the surveillance teams pass you, and keep track of you from up ahead.

'You won't know when we're following you,' Alroe warned me with a devilish grin. By now, they had reasonable grounds to pull both the truck and the Audi over.

'The team had been communicating with each other constantly, and we decided to stop them. So I switched on my blue lights, pulled up next to the truck, and motioned for the driver to pull over.'

When the truck driver pulled over, Alroe jumped out of his car and identified himself. The driver turned out to be the only person in the cab.

'He told me his name was Lawrence Muroma, from Zimbabwe. And I told him that I had received information that there was abalone in his truck.'

Muroma denied that there was anything untoward about the truck, and allowed the Hawks' task team to search it.

'At the same time, my colleagues had pulled over the Audi, and brought the driver and car to the rest of the team at the truck.'

The Audi's driver was identified as Qingquan Feng, a Chinese national. At the time, Feng pretended not to be able to speak much English. During a search of his vehicle, the Hawks found R46 000 in cash. Feng couldn't explain why he had the money on him. Both drivers were adamant that they did not know each other.

Gideon believes the cash would, in all likelihood, have been bribe money. 'That money would have been used to pay their way across the border,' he said. 'Or perhaps to bribe a police officer at a roadblock. Unfortunately for Mr Feng, he hadn't counted on the Hawks already being on his trail.'

Meanwhile, Alroe had opened the back of the truck.

'Inside we found a whole lot of plastic rolls. Huge rolls of bubble wrap. Each one about the height of a grown man,' he told me. 'It was the kind of plastic you use to wrap around fridges or microwaves when you transport it. I asked him again, anything illegal in here? And he just kept denying, denying.'

Alroe and the team were able to move the plastic rolls easily, but they found nothing illegal inside. Even after they'd emptied the whole cargo load, they'd still found nothing.

'And there was nothing else in there. But then we noticed, looking at the truck from the back, something funny sticking out next to the taillights. And we felt around there, and we found the bolts.'

He said you could see by the look in the two drivers' eyes that the team had found what they were looking for.

'I asked Lawrence what it was, but he said no no no, he had no idea. But when we had those bolts loose, the whole tailpiece of the truck body could be lifted, and we found a huge hidden compartment.'

The compartment was filled with rectangular brown boxes, each about a metre long.

'I asked the driver again, and he just bowed his head, shaking it. He didn't say a word.'

The Hawks removed the first box and opened it in Muroma's presence. It was filled to the brim with dried abalone.

'We had no idea if there was anyone else with the two men. Like I've told you, they always move in large groups, with their surveillance, always armed. So for everyone's safety, we arrested both men right there on the spot, and took them and the truck to the nearest police station in Philadelphia.'

Once there, both men were charged and processed.

'That's when the work started. The brown boxes were packed tightly into this hidden compartment that ran the whole length of the bottom of the truck. It was only a few centimetres high.'

The Hawks had to find someone small enough to fit into the tiny space, to get to all the boxes. Eventually, the job was given to a colleague who was small in stature.

'He had to physically climb in there. And we had to tie ropes to his feet, to pull him back out the deeper he went. In the end, we had to stop, because he nearly got stuck.'

The police on the scene ended up using a grinder to cut open the bottom of the truck, to get to all the boxes. After all the boxes were eventually removed, every abalone had to be counted and noted.

'We found more than 24 000 individual abalones, they weighed 1,396 tonnes. And they had a street value of R9,9 million.'

If you had to lay each piece out side by side, together they would take up 612 square metres. You could fit about 84 Citi Golfs into that same space.

'Muroma couldn't provide any good explanations for his illicit cargo. He just said that he was to drive the truck to Musina.'

Both men were kept overnight and appeared in court the following day. They were denied bail. Meanwhile, investigators started looking into their backgrounds.

'Muroma told us that he had started working for a company called Mega Chemicals two months before his arrest.'

But Mega Chemicals, which was supposedly registered in Zimbabwe, didn't seem to exist other than on paper. It was simply a front. A background check on Qingquan Feng revealed that he had a criminal record.

'And we saw that he had been arrested in 2016 on another case involving abalone. The case was at that time still ongoing in court.'

Feng's cellphone also contained incriminating evidence. Aside from the many photos of abalone in his picture gallery, his call records showed that he and Lawrence Muroma had been in constant contact. Which waylaid their story that they'd never met.

'Feng kept pretending that he couldn't speak English. He said so at his first court appearance. But we found voice notes from him to Lawrence where he was speaking English. He said things like Lawrence, why did you oversleep?' Alroe said.

The photos found on his phone were equally damning. They showed the washing and drying process the abalone had undergone, but also how the same boxes that were found on the truck were weighed and packed.

'Muroma had told us that he'd only been working for Mega Chemicals for two months, but we found evidence that he'd crossed the border back and forth between South Africa and Zimbabwe about nine times since November 2020. In the same truck,' Alroe laughed.

The warrant officer took his investigation one step further, and he was able to find evidence linking the truck and the Audi to each other on other occasions too. 'We obtained images from traffic-monitoring cameras mounted next to the highways that showed both vehicles travelling together on several other occasions. They crossed the border at Beitbridge to Zimbabwe together. Each time there was about a seven-day delay between the trips. Now remember, it takes between five and eight days to dry the abalone once it's removed from the ocean,' he said. 'So that painted the picture, while they took one shipment across the border, the next shipment was being readied.'

One truck and an Audi were making millions. It's likely that every cross-border trip also contained tonnes of a precious natural resource that is under threat along our coastline.

It was far from Alroe's biggest bust yet, but this case is the perfect example of how, when the police are willing to go the extra mile, they can have a powerful impact in the fight against organised crime.

Faced with the overwhelming evidence against them, both men plead guilty to charges related to the illegal possession and transportation of abalone. Lawrence Muroma was sentenced to eight years' imprisonment, and Qingquan Feng got seven years.

'It's the kind of sentence we hope sends out a message to the underworld,' Alroe told me.

A week after I left Cape Town, there were several murders, and alleged hits, that took place in the abalone underworld, probably orchestrated by rival gangs sorting out their differences. Safely back in my home in Pretoria, I couldn't help but spare a thought for the Hawks' members who have to enter that often dangerous alternate reality daily.

'It's not getting easier,' Alroe had said, wrapping up our conversation. 'It's getting more difficult. We're threatened often. It's not easy to think you're going to the shop to pick up bread, but you have to keep peering over your shoulder. These are hardened criminals we're dealing with. But it's a team effort. They have their gangs, we have our colleagues. As long as we stay positive, and work together, we'll win the war.'

9

PARA BELLUM

South Africa's police are neither trained nor equipped for conventional warfare. Yet certain units' daily operations involve the same threats that soldiers will face on a battlefield. This may sound like an exaggeration – but let's talk again when you've finished this chapter, dear reader.

I'd arranged to meet the members of TOMS at a safe house they sometimes use on the outskirts of Benoni. TOMS is short for Technical Operations Management Services. They are the Hawks' very own SWAT team – only better, in my opinion. They're SWAT on steroids. What they may lack in equipment and resources, they make up for in pure guts and operational skill.

After being buzzed through a large steel security gate, I swung left and parked in front of the boardroom where I was met by Brig. Frik Smith, Capt. Gert de Klerk and former captain Fred Hicks. Frik is currently the commanding officer of the TOMS' unit, and Gert is a long-time member. Fred used to be part of a similar but smaller team in the SAPS Serious Violent Crimes Unit in Gauteng. I was surprised to see Fred, a policeman I had incredible respect for when he was still a serving member. He'd been a key figure in pulling off an exposé I'd worked on many years earlier, and one of the few SAPS members willing to help me at the time.

'Don't tell me you've worked alongside these guys as well?' I asked, trying not to wince as my hand was shaken in his vice-like grip.

'Of course. I couldn't let them have all the fun.'

It's the typically nonchalant kind of banter I've often heard among men who risk their lives every other day to make a living. But make no mistake, when TOMS goes operational, it's no joke.

During his nineteen years in the SAPS, Gideon Jones dealt with a lot of violent crime. But he believes South African criminals have become particularly dangerous in the past few decades. 'I think that's the one thing that has increased with time, the levels of danger you encounter with crime. Today's criminals are well armed, and they won't hesitate to attack or resist the police.'

I have to agree. It seems hardly a day goes by without some video clip surfacing on social media as a testament to that statement. Running gun battles in our streets, hitmen firing point-blank at unsuspecting victims – the violence is overwhelming. This is not just my perception – try reading through South Africa's annual crime statistics sometime. The situation is abysmal.

So, when the Hawks need help to arrest the most danger-ous criminals the country has to offer, they call upon units like TOMS.

'We're a tactical unit,' Frik tells me. He's a tall man who wears his salt-and-pepper hair in a crew cut. Seeing him dressed in a dark suit and red pinstripe tie, I had the feeling he would look equally at home in a military uniform. He just has that air about him. 'We play a supporting role to DPCI units in all eleven provinces. As well as other ad hoc units.'

TOMS has been mandated to fulfil three core functions, he tells me. 'Our first role is to provide operational support to other Hawks' units. Mostly in what we call takedown operations. So we'll be the team who make the arrests on high-risk cases.'

Their second mandate is to handle the arrests of any criminals who end up on South Africa's most wanted lists, and similarly help law enforcement agencies like Interpol to catch criminals and international fugitives who've made their way to our shores.

'And our final mandate is the nationwide escorting of high-profile criminals, from the prisons to courts and back, for instance. Especially those cases where there are serious risks to contend with.'

In South Africa, one of the most dangerous categories or groups of criminals is the cash-in-transit (CIT) gangs. CIT robberies usually involve large groups of armed men attacking the armoured vehicles used by the banks to transport large amounts of cash. These are the people who are after the big money. And who are willing to risk anything to get it.

'Those are planned operations,' Gideon told me. 'They are planned and executed just like any military operation. And there are always high levels of violence involved in their plans.'

For the Hawks, who were specifically created to investigate priority crimes, these are right at the top of their list. 'It has been declared as a priority crime, and we have been given the sole mandate to investigate these crimes,' Frik told me.

But Anni, who has met and evaluated some of the most feared cash-in-transit robbers in jails across the country, says that's easier said than done. 'The problem is the amount of people involved. These gangs operate in big numbers. And when I say gang, I don't mean in the traditional sense of the word.'

She's found that the syndicates operate in loose groupings of individuals. They won't have the common structure of a boss, underboss and loyal followers. 'They'll farm out the work on a per-job basis. In Gauteng, they might use Mr X as a driver, but in KZN they'll use Mr Y. That makes the Hawks' job all the more difficult,' she said.

With his shaven head, neatly trimmed goatee and thickset muscular build, Capt. Gert de Klerk could pass for a member of some notorious biker club if you put him in the right outfit. He even has the gravelly, deep voice to suit the role. Appearances aside, he is a formidable policeman with years of experience under his belt in the TOMS' unit.

'You're not going to easily identify the guys at the top,' he told me. 'So we have to employ all sorts of strategies, and certain technologies, a lot of surveillance, to be successful.'

The Hawks, and especially TOMS, are not keen on discussing what exactly those strategies and technologies are. Rightfully so: in the war on the syndicates, they need every advantage they can get. But Frik didn't mind giving me an overview.

'How it typically works is information comes to our team, and there are mainly two ways that it comes to us. Information is generated by our team, and we are currently a group of about 40 people, or we'll get information from Crime Intelligence or private security companies. And that's when we investigate further or operationalise a takedown.'

Fred is the kind of man you can rely on to take control of any situation. He seems to run on adrenaline, so I wasn't surprised to learn that he now worked in the private security industry. These days he coordinates the investigations into courier hijackings for a large industry role player. This is another crime that's on the rise in South Africa as more and more people make use of online delivery services.

I first met him in 2018, working on an exposé of a dangerous kidnapping and extortion syndicate operating in the Vaal area. We'd had several complaints from members of the public who'd suffered extremely traumatic experiences at the hands of this gang.

After meeting with a few of the gang's previous victims, I had a clear picture of their MO. The victims had all advertised their vehicles, mostly double-cab bakkies, as for sale on the then-popular classifieds website OLX. They'd all been contacted by a man who told them the same story.

Speaking Afrikaans, the man had said he was a truck driver from Namibia, and that he worked for a diamond mine. He'd said he was interested in buying their vehicles and lured them to Vanderbijlpark with the promise that he would buy the vehicle with cash, provided he could see it first. The man created a false sense of urgency, saying that he was only in the country for a week and couldn't travel to the sellers since he only had his employer's truck to use.

On arrival in Vanderbijlpark, the seller would be met by the caller and introduced to a second member of the syndicate, supposedly a friend of the caller's. This man would show the victims a bag full of cash and some diamonds. The victims were told the sale of the diamonds would make up for the rest of the cash needed to buy their vehicles.

The victims were then taken to a nearby house to wait for the rest of the cash to arrive. Instead of getting paid, though, their lives would soon turn into violent ordeals.

In every case, men dressed in police uniforms then barged into the house, guns drawn. The victims were accused of being involved in illicit diamond deals. They were told they'd be held without bail, kept in cells full of dangerous criminals, and in all likelihood raped or tortured by their cellmates.

After being separated and bombarded by these kinds of threats, the victims were eventually offered a way out of their predicament. They had to hand over their ATM card PIN codes, and the login details to their banks. Other members of the gang would then empty their accounts.

In one case I looked into, a father and son had been lured into this intricately planned web of deceit. When the father refused to pay the bribe, the gang dropped all pretences and forced a gun into his mouth. He was told that both him and his son had seconds to live unless they cooperated. Like any father would, he gave in. The gang later forced him to accompany some of them to the local branch of his bank, where he had to withdraw the remaining funds from his account after his ATM card had reached its daily withdrawal limit. All this while his son was being held at gunpoint back at the house. All the victims were later released.

Since the police weren't making much headway at the time, we'd decided to shine the media spotlight on the gang and their activities. And I planned to lure them into a web of deceit of my own. I created a fake profile on OLX, offering a white double-cab bakkie for sale. It's not often that these kinds of attempts work, but the journalism gods must have been smiling down on me that day. About 48 hours later, the first (and only, by the way) call I received paid off.

The man on the other end of the line spoke Afrikaans (interesting) and said he was a truck driver for a diamond mine (oh really?) from Namibia (you don't say). He would only be in the country for a week (shame) but would pay cash for my vehicle if I could come show it to him in Vanderbijlpark (gotcha).

We agreed to meet at a petrol station in Vanderbijlpark a few days later. Ordinarily, we'd pitch up with our presenters and camera crew at the meeting and expose the man behind the calls. But these guys would most likely be armed and dangerous, and there was a significant risk that things might get out of hand. So, we decided to approach the police for their help.

That posed its challenges. At the time, we had no idea whether the police who entered the house were criminals dressed like police or actual members of the SAPS. But after making a few phone calls, I was told that Capt. Fred Hicks was the man to speak to. At the time, he was working Trio Crimes with a crack squad of fellow officers. They had a reputation for getting the job done.

Despite taking quite a lot of flak for it from his superiors at the time, he agreed to help us. On the morning I was supposed to meet the gang to show them my vehicle, we met him and his squad outside their offices near Krugersdorp.

The team were in bulletproof vests, and they'd brought big guns. We travelled in convoy to Vanderbijlpark, and a final briefing took place next to the road just a few minutes before the meeting.

One of Fred's men would play my role, and a second team member would play a friend who'd just come along for the ride. Luckily, the gang member had never met me in person, so we'd hoped he wouldn't have the faintest idea that he was speaking to somebody new. Our team would join other members of the police in a separate vehicle to observe from a distance.

At the agreed time, the two policemen met the gang member, and he climbed into their vehicle. As they drove off, they were under constant surveillance by other members of the Trio team. The police wanted to let the undercover operation go as far as it could without endangering their members' lives. But those plans soon changed, as we were informed by two-way radio that the bakkie was being tailed by a black vehicle that was acting suspiciously. Not knowing if the vehicle posed a threat to the undercover policemen in the bakkie, Fred made the call to pull the plug on the sting side of the operation.

In a matter of seconds, his team had arrested the suspect in the bakkie but also forced the black vehicle to a stop on one of the main roads of the small town, expertly taking control of the four suspects inside. The vehicle was searched and the bag of cash and the diamonds the gang had planned to use were found. To our surprise, both the cash and diamonds turned out to be ruses. The bundles of supposed R100 notes were simply blue cardboard that had a single real note attached to the top. The diamonds were fake.

Five people were arrested that day, among them Namibian nationals. As I'm writing this in 2023, the case against the syndicate we'd dubbed the OLX gang is still ongoing in the Palm Ridge court in Johannesburg. After our story aired, the police had completed separate investigations – and a total of nine suspects were eventually charged for the crimes. Two of the accused are indeed police officers.

So, I've seen Fred in action first-hand. That day in Vanderbijlpark was a masterclass in how a small, well-trained group of officers can take control of a dangerous group of criminals. Without a single shot being fired. But when it comes to CIT syndicates, even men who possess formidable policing skills are swimming against the tide.

'These guys don't care if there are innocent bystanders,' Fred told me. 'They'll hit a truck in broad daylight on a busy highway. They'll have explosives and open fire with assault rifles. We need to think twice before returning fire – we need to check where the public is and where the guards who were driving the cash truck are. They don't have those responsibilities and they don't care. They don't care who gets caught up in the crossfire.'

To understand why it's such an incredibly dangerous crime, and why it often turns deadly, you first need to understand how the typical CIT robbery goes down.

Firstly, there are two kinds of CIT heists. The police often refer to them as either cross-pavement or CIT. A cross-pavement robbery is when the gangs strike as bags of cash are being carried by the armoured van personnel from a shop where they've just collected the money to the armoured car. Armed men will approach the guards, guns drawn, and rob them of the cash. Although as common as the bigger CIT robberies, these are slightly less violent and often carried out by smaller groups of criminals.

But the big CIT robberies, where the syndicates target the actual armoured vehicles carrying the cash, are another story altogether. As Gideon told me, 'You'll see they are almost always carried out in the same ways. They have the same MO. Why? Because it works.'

The heists start with intelligence gathering. The gangs spend weeks and even months planning the robberies. They'll use every trick in the organised crime book to get the information they need to pull off the heists. This could include bribery, extortion, or threats. Fred says that during surveillance operations on the gangs, they've sometimes followed members to three different provinces in a single day.

'They'll spend days scouting routes, checking out the armoured trucks. From day to day, they drive from town to town, following up on their intelligence. And on the days that the robberies will occur, they'll have three jobs lined up for that day. So if the one doesn't work, they'll go for the next one.'

The intelligence comes from a so-called finger-man.

'In their structures,' Frik said, 'they will usually have one or two coordinators who have to get the information. And they get that information from the finger-man. He's someone who is actually in the armoured car or someone who works at the cash depot where they are going to pick up the money. Sometimes at the banks. But there's always a finger-man involved.'

It's the old story of organised crime not being able to exist without corruption. The finger-men are the insiders who can tell the gangs which routes the cash vans will take, and on which days they'll be loaded with the most money.

'They'll put just as much time and effort into planning an operation as we will,' Gert said, adding, 'No one knows how much money is in the vehicle on any given day. Sometimes it will only be one or two million rand. But then you'll see when they've hit a truck, then you'll see they had R5 million,

R10 million, R30 million in the truck. That information . . . sometimes the crew in the truck don't even have that information, but the finger-man inside the cash depot knows.'

On the day of the heist, the next step will be to get the armoured truck to come to a standstill. This is also where the violence starts.

'So the gangs will have between 10 and 30 men at their disposal,' Frik said. 'The advance team's job will be to shoot at the tyres of the cash van, to get it to stop in that way. Or they'll use their vehicles to ram it. Either from the front or the side.'

I've seen footage of an armoured car being hit by one of these ramming vehicles in a head-on collision. It's crazy – there's no other way to describe it. One minute the crew were just driving along, the next they'd been hit by a car I'd estimate was travelling upwards of 100 km/h. The damage inflicted on the armoured van was immense. Even if the crew weren't severely injured in the collision, there was no way the truck was going anywhere.

Gert says the individuals who do the ramming are hand-picked. 'You need someone who knows how to do it. That's why I've said, these guys all have their specific expertise. There was this one guy who only used high-end Mercedes-Benz vehicles to do the job. And you knew if you found that type of Mercedes at the scene, then it was him.'

The vehicles used are in most cases stolen or hijacked, and they are high-performance models with plenty of safety features.

'If I'm going to ram an armoured truck,' he continued, 'I'm not going to do it in a little Nissan 1400. I'm going to hit them with a car that I know at least has airbags, it's relatively safe, and I'll be able to go and enjoy my money afterwards.'

Once they've brought the vehicle to a standstill, another team, who would have been following along in separate vehicles, will jump into action. In most cases, they'll be armed with high-powered automatic assault rifles, like AK-47s or police- and military-issue R4s and R5s.

'They'll order the driver and crew out of the vehicle,' Fred said. 'And if they resist, the shooting starts. And if they still don't want to get out, they'll bring in the explosives guy.'

Often, the explosives expert won't even be on the scene during the first few minutes of the heist. Once the truck has been brought to a standstill, he's phoned and brought in by car.

'He'll come in,' Fred continued, 'he sticks his explosives to the cab of the truck, and he blows it open. And after that he leaves the scene again, his part of the job is done, and he'll share in the spoils later.'

The explosives are often obtained from the mining industry, from which they've been either stolen or bought through nefarious means. This all happens on public roads, posing tremendous danger to innocent bystanders caught up in the incidents. I've been at the scene of a heist during the operation. There is nothing quite like the sound of an AK-47 set to rapid fire to make the hairs on the back of your neck stand to attention. Or the incredible sight of a steel-reinforced armoured truck being blown apart as if it were made of little more than papier-mâché. The accompanying eardrum-violating sonic boom can be heard kilometres away.

During the heist, the syndicate will also have shooters on the scene, men well versed in the use of the automatic rifles they carry. Their job will be to deal with any resistance the gang faces. Many of them will have some kind of military experience and will have proven records of staying calm under fire. With the kind of planning involved and the handpicked expertise, the gangs are a force to be reckoned with.

'They'll choose the vehicles, the drivers,' Gert told me. 'They'll say okay, give me two guys from Gauteng as drivers. And I want three shooters from Mpumalanga. And that's how they'll combine them. Because they know at the end of the day, if the shooter from Mpumalanga gets caught, he'll only be able to ID his two friends from Mpumalanga.'

The heists are usually over in a matter of minutes. Speed is essential if the gangs hope to evade the authorities. Once they've blown open the armoured cab, they'll grab as much of the loot as they can and make their getaway in high-performance vehicles. Often, the vehicles used to ram the armoured car are set alight, effectively destroying any possible evidence that could identify the gang members in a fiery inferno.

The gangs don't hesitate to use violent tactics to protect themselves, and ordinary police responding to these scenes are often outgunned. You simply can't expect soft-skinned patrol vehicles, each usually only manned by two police officers carrying 9mm pistols, to be effective against a group of twenty men armed with assault rifles. Gideon knows that feeling all too well: 'This is not an ordinary guy in the street you want to catch. This is like a military operation that's been planned against you. It's as if you're going after a well-trained unit of soldiers. And they have more firepower than you. And the truth is, we can't expect our police to be soldiers, they aren't trained for warfare. But taking on these gangs is like going into open combat.'

In 2019, the TOMS' team started an investigation into one of the major syndicates behind CIT heists at the time.

'I was contacted by Crime Intelligence,' Gert said. 'And a DPCI unit in Pietermaritzburg. They were looking at this gang that was made of people from KZN, Gauteng, Mpumalanga and the Eastern Cape.'

The gang were suspected of having committed several CIT robberies in both Gauteng and KwaZulu-Natal. When members of Crime Intelligence and the SAPS Special Task Force (another specialised unit similar to TOMS but which falls directly under the SAPS) tried to arrest the suspects, a massive shootout occurred.

'One CI [Crime Intelligence] member was wounded, and another killed during the shooting. And one task force member was killed during the incident,' Gert explained.

The teams involved had received information about a possible CIT being planned, and while following up on the information they had unwittingly driven into the middle of a CIT heist in progress. 'They didn't know where it was going to go down, and they were tracking the suspects. And the next thing they drove into the CIT. And the gang turned around and opened fire on the police,' Gert said. 'So when they contacted me, the information was that many of the role players had fled back to the Gauteng area after the shooting.'

Gert and the TOMS' team, coordinating with Hawks' members in KwaZulu-Natal, started their investigations by activating every source and confidential informant they could think of.

'We managed to track down some of the suspects. There were also quite a few firefights that broke out when we tried to arrest them. But we had quite a few successes.'

Realising that the police were hot on their heels, the original gang involved in the KZN heist broke up into splinter groups.

'These guys don't have jobs, don't have permanent homes,' Fred said. 'They're always ready to move to the next job. So when they scatter, it's often difficult to trace them. They have money and street smarts. They just disappear.'

But soon, Gert told me, the TOMS' team had fresh leads.

'We got intel that some of these guys, who were part of a splinter group that had gone to ground in the East Rand, were planning a CIT in Mahikeng. So we mobilised along the route they were going to use, we had observation points and stopper groups.'

'Stopper group' is a military term, but in CIT heists they're used by both the police and the criminals. In general, it refers to a group of soldiers who have been placed along a route to block off a specific road or area.

'And we had three or four cash vans come past us and nothing happened. There was no sign of the criminals,' Gert said. 'But then a G4S van passed, and there was an attempt to rob it.'

The TOMS' team were further down the road, and members of the Special Task Force were first on the scene.

'The task force members came under fire, and they retaliated. During the shootout, some of the suspects fled in vehicles.'

In the ensuing chaos, TOMS' members were involved in a high-speed pursuit of some of the suspects. 'And they were shooting at our team during this car chase. Unfortunately, Detective Warrant Officer Delene Grobler-Koonin was hit. And she passed away on the scene,' Gert said.

The men and women who work in specialised units like TOMS confront danger daily. It comes with the territory. Facing and surviving the constant threats together creates an extremely deep bond between them. When they lose one of their own, it's an incredibly personal loss. For the trio of tough operators telling me the story that day, it certainly wasn't easy to discuss. But their faces told you everything you needed to know.

Gideon had shared a thought-provoking idea on the subject with me. 'The problem is that person knows he's committed several violent crimes. He knows he could receive lifelong sentences for the crimes he's committed. So to shoot someone is going to make no difference to any sentence he might be given. You know if you've pulled off twenty heists, how much prison time can you receive? Twenty life sentences? What would a murder add to that?'

But Detective Warrant Officer Grobler-Koonin wasn't the only team member the Hawks would lose that day. Gert sighed deeply as he continued the story, valiantly hiding the turbulent emotions he was reliving.

'We had information that some of the suspects were headed towards Coligny,' he said. Coligny is a small maize farming town in the North West province. 'In Coligny, our TOMS' team spotted a suspicious Kombi. When our members approached the Kombi, the occupants opened fire. Detective Warrant Officer Wynand Herbst was wounded in the ensuing gunfight, and later on, he succumbed to his injuries on the way to the hospital.'

The gunfight, which had occurred near a petrol station in Coligny, left three of the suspects dead, while two others were arrested. The Hawks seized three AK-47 rifles, two pistols, 86 rounds of ammunition and two vehicles.

To prevent any legal complications, I won't be naming any of the criminals involved in this case. They're all still facing the charges against them in court. But one of the men arrested in Coligny at the time, Jabulani Moses Yika (41), has been sentenced to 30 years of effective imprisonment for his role in the heist that day.

'It's always heartbreaking to lose one of your own,' Frik told me. 'But on that day in 2020, to lose two members in one day, it was tragic.' Rifling through some of the newspaper clippings about the operation, he was still looking at some of the headlines when he continued, 'You know, in our work we leave home in the morning and we plan an operation, but there are no guarantees that you're coming home tonight.'

Even the usually stoic Fred struggled to express his feelings on the subject.

'It's a terrible feeling,' he said, drawing a deep breath in before he continued, 'to suddenly lose someone that you know very well . . . You know that person has a family and children. You have children, so you can just imagine what they are going through. And then to go and give them this kind of news . . . '

By June 2020, two months after the Mahikeng heist, ten of the suspects had been accounted for. Three of them were fatally wounded in the shootouts with police, and seven had been arrested. The rest had gone to ground, with the Hawks continuing their investigations.

'We followed up on a variety of leads because some of the suspects were still on the loose,' Gert told me. 'But these guys had gone deep cover, they knew they were wanted.'

In the end, it was Fred who got a tip-off about a group of suspects who were about to pull off a CIT robbery on the East Rand. This led the team to a final explosive confrontation with the same gang.

'We had information that our outstanding suspects, and new team members they had recruited, were holed up in a safe house in a suburb called Dalpark,' Fred said. 'And they were about to pull off a robbery the next morning. So I phoned Gert and said, please come and help us, I'm putting a team together on my side. I had guys from the East Rand Trio unit, competent people. So we would be a large group. Because the information we had was that there were about 20, 25 people in the safe house.'

'I got the call at about 2 a.m.,' Gert recalled. 'And me and my team headed out to Dalpark. We met Captain Hicks and his men about 1,5 km from the safe house.'

Operations like these are bread and butter for specialised units like TOMS. They're also a tactical nightmare, Gideon had told me. 'These guys are holed up in an urban area, surrounded by other houses and innocent civilians,' he said. 'And that's what the gang wants, anonymity. But it's very challenging for the police.'

On top of that, the police can't just enter the premises with guns blazing – they are there to arrest the suspects, and they have to allow them to surrender.

'Let's be honest,' Gideon said. 'When you look at this syndicate and the previous incidents, how many police hadn't they already killed? There was no question that they would shoot. Absolutely no question. So put yourself in the shoes of the police who have to go in there. How brave do you need to be to walk into a house, knowing they are going to shoot at you, probably with AK-47s?'

The team sent in observers to scout the area and gather as much intel as possible about the house. 'I drove past the place with two team members,' Fred said. 'And as we drove back down, we passed it again. A taxi entered the premises. The registration number traced back to an incident we had in Pretoria, with the same group. So we knew it was them,' he said. As they prepared to approach the house, the teams were split up into tactical units. 'We posted our people according to what we needed. So we placed stopper groups to close off the roads and to keep the public out. Some team members were to approach the house from the side, others from the back. And then the main group who would do the penetration.'

Before they attempt these kinds of operations, his team will have the necessary search or arrest warrants.

'You don't want to go in there with someone you're in doubt about,' Fred said. 'That's why we work with handpicked individuals. You need to trust the guy next to you. You need to know he's not going to turn and run when the shooting starts. Or even worse, phone them and warn them that we're coming. Then by the time we get there, the place is abandoned. And you only find their cars. I know that many policemen see it as a success to find some stolen cars. But it's better to catch the suspects.'

Most AK-47s use 20- or 30-round magazines. Chambered in 7,62 × 39 mm cartridges that travel at 715 metres per second, they can fire about 100 rounds a minute in fully automatic mode. At close range, they are deadly. The police entering the house that day would have known that the chances of surviving a burst of the deadly weapon's fire were slim. But they didn't let that stop them.

'As we moved down the road,' Gert said, 'and we got close to the gate, one of the observers came on the radio and said, listen, the Kombi has been started.'

The first group of robbers had been on their way to get into position for the CIT they had planned later that day.

'And as they were about to exit through the gate we came across each other,' Gert smiled wryly. 'We identified ourselves and told them to stop. And that's when they started shooting.'

As both sides dove for cover, the shooting between the two groups intensified. Some of the syndicate members tried to flee out the back of the house, where they ran into the waiting Hawks' members. The scene was absolute chaos.

'They know if we arrest them they're going to jail for a long time,' Fred said. 'So when you go in there you need to be prepared, you can't run away from them. Because if you run away or doubt in yourself, it's going to cost your colleague's life, or yours.'

As the men in the taxi drew back towards two outside garages on the property, the police teams closed in from all sides.

'The front entry team made it inside quite quickly because the gate was still open from when they were about to leave,' Fred said. 'And then we all just pushed in. And it was quite a gun battle between the two sides. Some of our guys were even injured from shrapnel caused by the shattering concrete as the bullets flew.'

Gert told me that the saying 'no plan survives first contact with the enemy' may be clichéd, but this doesn't make it any less true. 'You have to adapt or die, you have to make split-second decisions. Bullets are flying everywhere. And it becomes a situation of survival.'

As the teams got close to the house, they threw flash grenades inside to disorientate their attackers.

'Let me tell you,' Fred laughed, 'if you're inside a room where one of those goes off, you're going to regret it.' It's not a pleasant experience, I've been told, and it gave the officers precious seconds to enter the premises in relative safety. 'If you have to enter a house full of bad guys, it's the thing to use,' he smiled.

It was only afterwards, once the Local Criminal Record Centre (LCRC) crime scene investigators were combing through the aftermath of the scene, that the TOMS' team were told of another brush with death they'd unwittingly had that morning.

'One of the grenades had landed on this bag,' Gert said. 'And it had rolled off and exploded, causing the distraction we had needed. But later on, the forensics guys told us that bag had been full of explosives.'

The explosives would most likely have been used later that day to blow open the armoured vehicle the gang had targeted.

'And those explosives had been prepped, they were connected to wires . . . ' Fred recalled. 'And afterwards we were like, this could have gone south very quickly. If that had gone off, that would have been a real surprise for us all. Not just for them, but for us also.'

Luckily, that hadn't happened – and the police teams were able to overpower the gang, most of them eventually surrendering.

'And at the end of the day, we arrested nineteen suspects. Two of them were shot and killed during the shootout,' Fred said. None of the police suffered any major injuries. Among the nineteen arrested were the final outstanding members of the syndicate the TOMS' members had been after for years. Police also recovered three AK-47s, two R5 rifles, two pistols and the explosives. But even this victory was bittersweet.

'Two or three of them had managed to escape in the chaos of the takedown,' Gert told me. 'Later on that day, we were told that a woman had been hijacked nearby shortly after our operation.'

It turned out that the innocent member of the public had run into the fleeing CIT robbers, and they'd forced her out of her car at gunpoint. While they made their getaway, they were spotted on the highway and pulled over by a SAPS Highway Patrol vehicle that had noticed their reckless driving.

'And after they were pulled over, they shot and killed the officer who had stopped them.'

The policeman on duty that day was Constable George Molefi, a well-liked and respected member of the Gauteng Highway Patrol.

'From there they hijacked a passing courier vehicle and took the driver hostage. They took him to Soweto where they let him go.'

The men have since been arrested and charged, and are currently awaiting trial.

'I think these levels of cold-bloodedness,' Gideon mused, 'you usually find in your worst international drug cartels, you don't usually see it playing out every other day. This is so far past the realms of normality. It truly is an abnormal situation.'

Despite the danger, it was the kind of work Fred enjoyed most during his time in the police: 'It's when you have milliseconds to make decisions when the bullets are flying around you, that's the best part of that type of work.' Perhaps noticing my incredulous expression after that surprising comment, he continued, 'I'm sure many people will disagree with me, but those moments of stress there, those are the moments that make the job fun. And when you know you've won. That's the cherry on the cake,' he finished. And to tell you the truth, I think I've got to know him well enough to believe he meant every word.

In March 2023, the Minister of Police awarded special commendations to each individual involved in the Dalpark case.

'That evening,' Frik said, 'the minister told us that we are the final thin blue line that can still make a difference in the war against organised crime. And we can't fail.'

Back when I was finishing off going through the case with Gideon, we'd been going through some of the newspaper clippings together. Every headline seemed to scream danger. Words like 'deadly gun battle' and 'bullets fly along R101' were printed across the pages, while pictures of bullet-riddled vehicles and bloodied corpses provided a sombre reminder of the gruesome trail left in the CIT gang's wake.

'You know what?' he said, pointing to a picture of Gert leading a handcuffed suspect down a road. 'These guys are unsung heroes. They really are. It is heroic to go in every time, day after day, year after year, and get involved in those kinds of confrontations. They all deserve some kind of medal for bravery.'

That's a sentiment I wholeheartedly agree with, and I caught myself wondering what Fred would say about it. Back in the boardroom where I'd met him and the TOMS' members, I'd conclude that these men were a special breed.

'You get guys who want to come and be part of these operations,' Fred had said. 'And they arrive with a big heart. But with the first contact, then everything changes. And that is unfortunately true. Luckily we have strong police members who can overcome this kind of thing, and that's what we want to do. Because one of these days it's my family who might become victims.'

I finished my interviews with Frik, Gert and Fred in early 2023. Since then, the TOMS' unit has had to deal with more losses. On 9 June 2023, TOMS' operative Sgt Leka Maja was shot and killed in Mamelodi when the Hawks went after a group of suspected CIT robbers who were hiding out in an informal dwelling in the township. Three of the suspects were also killed.

Just under three months later, on 1 September 2023, the TOMS' team, assisted by other specialised units, broke the back of a CIT syndicate that had been operating in the Limpopo area. During a gun battle that lasted for over an hour, TOMS' member Lt Col Joe Coetzer was badly wounded. He was lucky to survive but has had to have one of his legs amputated above the right knee. During the shootout, eighteen members of the CIT gang lost their lives. They were suspected of having taken part in at least eleven CITs in Limpopo in 2023. After the shootout, which took place in Louis Trichardt, four more suspects were arrested in Thohoyandou.

I don't think CIT robberies are going to disappear from our headlines anytime soon. There's simply too much money to be made, and the syndicates behind the crimes are getting increasingly sophisticated – and ever more ruthless. As we'd finished off our last conversation, Gert had squared his burly shoulders, straightening the black tactical jacket with the Hawks' emblem embroidered across his chest. The look on his face at that moment I can only describe as deadly determination.

'Crime catches up to you, always,' he'd said. 'You will get caught. And they better have eyes in the backs of their heads, because we'll be right behind them.'

Acknowledgements

I would like to extend my deepest gratitude to the Hawks National Head Lieutenant General (Dr/Adv) Godfrey Lebeya for green-lighting my request to tell some of the unit's stories, and allowing the South African public the opportunity to get a behind-the-scenes look at the critical work done by the Directorate for Priority Crime Investigation.

I also owe a huge debt of gratitude to Brigadier Thandi Mbambo and the rest of the DPCI's communications team for their invaluable help. Specifically, Colonel Katlego Mogale, Lieutenant Colonel Philani Nkwalase, Captain Lloyd Ramovha and Warrant Officer Zinzi Hani.

A very special thank you to Brigadier Frik Smith for his inputs.

A true crime book by its very nature requires a great deal of time and research. But it's not just the author's time we're talking about. The investigating officers you've got to know through these stories, and some of them who aren't mentioned here, all availed themselves freely – often while having to juggle ongoing investigations and court dates. For that, I thank you all from the bottom of my heart. In no particular order, they are: Warrant Officer Paul Holtzhausen, Captain Manie van Zyl, Lieutenant Colonel Erhard Stroh, Colonel Danie

Hall, the undercover agent I've called OG in this book (you know who you are), Warrant Officer Alroe Luiters, Colonel Jacques Visser, Captain Lizelle Herbst, Colonel Johan Jooste, Lieutenant Colonel Masenxani Chauke, Captain Corné de Bod (SAPS), ex-Captain Ben Booysen, Captain Karin du Plessis, Brigadier Frik Smith, ex-Captain Fred Hicks (SAPS), Captain Gert de Klerk, Brigadier Hennie Flynn and Warrant Officer Rassie Erasmus.

Many thanks also to Ernie van Rensburg, Albert Gryvenstein, Stacy Magid, George Moraitis and Carlos Ferreira for their time and patience, and for sharing their stories.

To my colleagues and close friends Professor Anni Hesselink and Gideon Jones, your time, experience and incredible insights into the underworld of crime meant so much to me – I am truly grateful.

No journalist would be successful without an extensive list of contacts and connections. You can only get so far without knowing people who know people . . . For their help in opening so many doors, a sincere thank you to Big Paul and Kurt Heydenrych.

Last but by no means least, a huge thank you to the incredible group of people over at Tafelberg and NB Publishers. I'm both humbled and grateful for your belief in and commitment to this book. Thank you to Robert Kaden at Media24 for the introductions. To both Carla Coetzee and Na'eemah Masoet who guided me along every step of the way, I owe a huge debt of gratitude. Angela Voges handled the editing – you are a star! Thank you also to Marthie Steenkamp for the design, Mike Cruywagen at Nudge Studio for the cover and Glynne Newlands for the proofing.

About the author

Born and raised in Pretoria, Graham Coetzer is an award-winning investigative journalist and television producer. His work has led him on many interesting adventures across the African continent and even further abroad.

When he's not being questioned at gunpoint about the reasons for carrying his camera gear into places like the Democratic Republic of the Congo, he spends most of his time working for South Africa's longest-running current affairs television show, *Carte Blanche*. So far, they've been kind enough to put up with him for thirteen years; he hopes to stay there for many more, doing what he loves best: exposing the people who scam, exploit, bully and otherwise do harm to ordinary South Africans.

He has a passion for fast cars and even faster motorcycles, and when he can afford to do so he races a little turbocharged Alfa Sud Sprint in local club events. When he's not driving fast or investigating the underworld, he likes to spend his time with his wife, daughters and the family's pet Pekingese – two dogs that he claims contribute absolutely nothing to society. But according to sources, he's been spotted sneaking them scraps from the table and even acting as their personal pillow when the trio spend lazy weekends together exploring a good book.